FEARLESS BY DESIGN

FEARLESS BY DESIGN

Proven Strategies for Overcoming Fear, Conquering Anxiety, and Excelling In Life

Tom Blackledge

ISBN: 978-1-7384274-0-6

www.TomBlackledge.com

DEDICATION

For my love.

PREFACE

"IT IS NOT THE CRITIC WHO COUNTS;
NOT THE MAN WHO POINTS OUT HOW
THE STRONG MAN STUMBLES, OR
WHERE THE DOER OF DEEDS COULD
HAVE DONE THEM BETTER. THE
CREDIT BELONGS TO THE MAN WHO IS
ACTUALLY IN THE ARENA, WHOSE
FACE IS MARRED BY DUST AND SWEAT
AND BLOOD; WHO STRIVES VALIANTLY;
WHO ERRS, WHO COMES SHORT AGAIN
AND AGAIN, BECAUSE THERE IS NO
EFFORT WITHOUT ERROR AND
SHORTCOMING; BUT WHO DOES
ACTUALLY STRIVE TO DO THE DEEDS;
WHO KNOWS GREAT ENTHUSIASMS,
THE GREAT DEVOTIONS; WHO SPENDS
HIMSELF IN A WORTHY CAUSE; WHO
AT THE BEST KNOWS IN THE END THE
TRIUMPH OF HIGH ACHIEVEMENT,
AND WHO AT THE WORST, IF HE FAILS,
AT LEAST FAILS WHILE DARING
GREATLY, SO THAT HIS PLACE SHALL
NEVER BE WITH THOSE COLD AND
TIMID SOULS WHO NEITHER KNOW
VICTORY NOR DEFEAT."

— Theodore Roosevelt

CONTENTS

INTRODUCTION

In 2002, Eminem released a track called "Lose Yourself" as part of the soundtrack for the movie *8 Mile*. The film depicted biographical moments of the artist's life, capturing his early days as a budding rapper and his stage performance before he became famous.

In the song, Eminem raps about the nerves he feels every time he waits to get on stage to perform and the stage fright that cripples him.

He's desperate to perform and put on a show. He knows it's his calling.

But every time he steps onto the stage, he's sick with nerves. He suffers from crippling stage fright. He struggles to remember his lyrics and stumbles on his journey to eventually becoming a great performing artist.

Obstacles and failures litter his path, but he knows he must overcome them all to fulfil his destiny.

It's not just about those massive moments of being on stage and performing like Eminem. We all face moments that stir the same feelings, no matter how significant they seem to others. It could be a job interview, a sporting event, a date, a meeting, a speaking engagement, a wedding, or a family gathering. I want everyone to feel they can face whatever is required of them and not only step up but also excel.

This book is, at its heart, about letting go.

Of opinions.

Of limiting beliefs.

Of fears.

Of judgement.

It offers real-life examples of strategies to guide you towards your dreams, giving you the champion's mindset you've always dreamt of. I hope you take away at least one actionable point from this book, a point that enables you to overcome your anxieties and fears and achieve your ambitious goals. Moreover, I hope it equips you to help others achieve their dreams too.

Through my life, from being one of the first fighters from the UK to compete in the renowned UFC, to coaching Special Forces units, to public speaking before businesses and sports teams, to working as a stuntman on a Hollywood blockbuster, I've learned what it takes to achieve deep-seated dreams. My aim in sharing these achievements isn't to brag but to demonstrate that I understand the challenges of reaching for what might seem unattainable.

As you delve into this book, each chapter is crafted to inspire and guide:

- **Chapter One** delves into my relationship with fear.
- **Chapter Two** warns of the negative effects of too much mainstream media on our mental health, conditioning us to live in various states of fear.
- **Chapter Three** explores how constantly being in this an anxious state affects our bodies and how we worsen this through imagined outcomes.
- **Chapter Four** addresses stressful work environments and the power of visualisation in moving our nervous systems to states of healthy balance.
- **Chapter Five** focuses on just how fully fear of failure can cripple our ability to move ahead.
- **Chapter Six** recounts a tale from my coaching career, discussing fear in athletes specifically, and looking at the disempowering nature of suspersitions.
- **Chapter Seven** reveals how our fear of success can be just as paralysing as fear of failure.

- **Chapter Eight** introduces problem-focused and emotion-focused coping mechanisms.
- **Chapter Nine** delves into the wisdom of Stoic philosophy and how we can apply it to mastering our own mindset.
- **Chapter Ten** highlights the transformative power of gratitude.
- **Chapter Eleven** showcases the art of reframing situations.
- **Chapter Twelve** underscores the importance of decisive action.
- **Chapter Thirteen** contrasts growth and fixed mindsets.
- **Chapter Fourteen** looks at the profound impact of physical actions like movement and breathing.
- **Chapter Fifteen** concludes the book, guiding you on implementing what you've learned.

I've made many mistakes in my journey, but they've been my greatest lessons. By opening up to you, I hope to inspire you to chase your dreams, no matter the obstacles.

If you enjoy this book, please visit my website, www.TomBlackledge.com, for regular updates and content. Enjoy.

CHAPTER 1
THE BEGINNING

*"The cave you fear to enter holds the
treasure you seek."*

Joseph Campbell

Mixed Martial Arts, or MMA for short, is a sport
where two athletes enter an octagon-shaped
caged arena, engaging in a fight to see who the
best combatant is. They use a myriad of skills,
techniques, and abilities to best their opponent
and emerge victorious. They can win through a
knockout (like in boxing from a head trauma),
submission (when the fighter is caught in a hold
that could cause serious injury), referee stoppage
(if the referee is concerned about one of the
fighters taking too much damage), or by a judges'
decision, where three judges sit cage-side,
scoring the fight on certain criteria.

Today, the sport is massive. It garners massive
pay-per-view numbers for superstars like Connor
McGregor and Ronda Rousey, numbers that rival
or surpass many mainstream sports. And with

organisations like the UFC, Bellator, PFL, and other big MMA promotions around the globe, opportunities are plenty for fans and athletes alike.

But my story starts long before the flashing lights of Las Vegas and packed stadiums of thirty thousand fans. In its infancy, the sport was vastly different than today. When I began my mixed martial arts career in the late 1990s and early 2000s, it wasn't the sport we see today. I use the term 'career' loosely because I didn't initially intend for it to become my career. At that time, the sport wasn't even called MMA. More commonly, it was referred to as NHB or no holds barred, meaning no hold or strike was illegal, a nod to its Brazilian roots in Vale Tudo, Portuguese for "anything goes."

The sport today is quite different from its origins, evolving over the years into a mainstream activity that allows athletes to earn recognition and financial success.

As a young martial artist, I would get every martial arts magazine I could. I'd read them cover to cover, absorbing all the knowledge they offered. I'd also stand in my local bookstore as a youngster, leafing through magazines I couldn't buy, just to gather any extra insight. By then, I'd watched the UFC and studied the styles of fighters like Royce Gracie and Ken Shamrock. I'd find tapes of these fights, imported from the US or

Russia, and watch them intently, trying to incorporate the best techniques into my practice.

By my late teens, I'd earned black belts in various martial arts disciplines and began to integrate these techniques into my training and some of my teaching. I also sparred with many of the door security staff in my town. These weren't just any bouncers; they were trained in martial arts and combat techniques essential for their jobs. And when I say I was fighting with them, I wasn't out on a night out causing a ruckus. We'd meet for organised spars, building relationships that remain strong today. Many of them later became my students, and I coached them for many fights.

Even with all this training and experience in various martial arts, I hadn't taken part in a real NHB fight, and I felt something was missing. Opportunities to fight were few and far between, not just in the UK. Then, in one of my martial arts magazines, I saw an advert. It showcased two fighters with a tagline, "Two men enter, one man leaves," and a form below asking for your name, age, and fighting experience.

I filled out the form, envisioning myself as the champion, trophy in hand, featured on the cover of a martial arts magazine. I enclosed a cheque for £25 – the fee to compete–and sent it off. But the moment I dropped it into the post box, the realisation of what I'd just done hit me in the gut instantly. I was going to fight another man in a no-holds-barred contest that I had signed a disclaimer form for. I'd given up all my claims of responsibility should an injury occur to me. Or even death. I've never felt nerves like this.

To say I was afraid would be a massive understatement. If I had been able to open that red post box and take back my application, I would have done so in a heartbeat.

I was a young, scared boy who was following his dreams into the unknown, and I was *terrified.*

No one I knew had travelled this road before, so I had to make the path for myself. I had to accept that the fight was happening and that I had committed to do it. But that didn't stop me from playing out scenarios in my head of all the ways I could avoid the fight.

I imagined the letter and cheque getting lost in the post. Maybe my opponent would be unavailable. Maybe my cheque would bounce. Maybe I'd get injured and have an understandable excuse to withdraw.

Whenever we put ourselves out there to being open to being vulnerable, we will clutch at ways to remove the fear to try to feel safe again. We don't realise that the way we build our resilience, our coping mechanisms, is by facing those things that terrify us . The adversity you face today, will create the resilience you need tomorrow.

If I had listened to these stories in my mind, these excuses, and acted upon them, they would have eaten at me forever.

Fear of outcomes and the pressure we put on ourselves to perform can cause that inner voice to talk to us in some strange ways.

Many fighters will have conversations with themselves about ways to get out of their upcoming bout, "If I crash my car and get hurt, I'll be out of the fight. Everyone would understand"

"If I'm injured from training, I could pull from the fight."

Even as close as fight night, as they are walking to their warm-up room, I've known fighters who think about tripping over a matted edge, rolling their ankle, and not being able to fight with a valid excuse.

Admittedly these thoughts are very fleeting, but It's very common. As we will see in a later chapter, even the very best in the world get these thoughts. They just embrace great coping mechanisms like the ones I'm going to coach you on to get through.

Once my cheque cleared, and everything was sorted, I received a letter with all the fight details. Back then, I didn't drive. So on fight night, I had to rely on a friend to get me there. These days, fighters usually arrive with their coach and a team, a vital support network that boosts their confidence as they prepare for the cage.

Back then, though, I didn't have a fight coach. I had a sensei. He taught me martial arts, but he wasn't into NHB or sport-style fighting, so it was my path to go down alone.

Off to the fight I went with a friend generously driving me to the venue. It was paradoxically the longest and shortest drive ever. I was desperate to get there and get it all over and done with, but frantically wanted to head back home and retreat to safety.

All those crazy ideas of crashing the car or getting hurt were popping into my head. My self-talk was all over the place, saying things like, "It's okay. You've competed before," and answering with, "But never to this extent. Never against guys like these."

The adrenaline was something I had never experienced before. The nerves nauseated me to the point that I couldn't stomach food. And constant images of the fight flashed up in my head.

This wasn't just on the journey to the fight. This had been happening for months and weeks prior.

I had lived the fight a thousand times in my mind. Seeing myself victorious. Seeing my opponent victorious. But every time, regardless of the perceived, visualised outcome, the fight thoughts consumed me and made me anxious.

When I became a full-time professional fighter, I realised this process was completely normal, and I got these feelings before every fight that ever meant anything to me.

I could be sleeping in the deepest of restful states, when out of the blue, in some dark corner of my mind, a voice would whisper, "Hey."

Dazed and confused, I would give a little attention to this little voice in my mind.

"Yes?" I would reply curiously.

"You know this fight?" It would ask.

Then . . . I'D BE WIDE AWAKE with images and visualisations running through my mind. Then the questions started.

Then what ifs.

What if he hits you harder than you have ever been hit?

Then imagined outcomes.

How will I react to losing?
How will I cope if I get hurt?

Then the judgements.

How will my friends react if I lose?
Will my family still love me?

Then failures.

How will I feel as a failure if I don't win?

Then successes.

I will be living life as a world-famous athlete, will I be able to maintain this lifestyle?

But they were all instrumental in helping to teach me the most valuable lessons that life and fear will offer. Lessons I will reveal to you as you read on, but for now, back to fight night.

When we arrived at the venue, a large, unassuming sports hall, we headed inside. I met with the promoter and organised details—tickets, fees, walkout music and where I will be warming up and getting ready to fight.

I headed into my locker room, got changed, and started jumping rope.

My friend left the room to walk around and check out the venue, as I sat on the bench in the changing room with my thoughts.

Alone.

Afraid.

I'd played this moment over in my head countless times daily, and it felt as awful as I had envisioned. The smell of the locker room. Pungent sweat and wintergreen oil. I sat there with the heaviest of legs, my heart racing, leaving me feeling nauseous. My body wasn't doing what I wanted, and I felt a ton of pressure. It sounds like an Eminem song, and to be fair, that's precisely what he was rapping about in his song "Lose Yourself" from the movie *8 Mile*—same predicament, different scenario, and none of mom's spaghetti.

Why did I say I would do this fight?

If I could go back now and take back that cheque, I would. If I could have clicked my fingers and magically transported from this locker room right now, I would have done it in an instant. I was a young boy, and I felt even younger, smaller, and more helpless than I ever had at that exact moment in time. I was terrified.

I'm not too proud or big to admit I had never been as scared or lonely in my life as I had at that exact moment. Being alone in that locker room in the eerie quiet and stillness showed me more of myself than I had ever seen before.

I felt like a gladiator in the ancient days of Rome, ready to do battle in the Colosseum in front of the bloodthirsty crowd. I could hear the roar of the crowd and the cheers and boos they emitted as their fighters won or lost, echoing slightly through the halls and corridors.

I started to move and limber up. I stretched and shadow-boxed. Then there was a knock at the locker room door. A head popped in as one of the event staff taped up my gloves. It was time.

I didn't know how to feel.

My heart felt like it was beating out my chest.

My breathing was erratic and all in my upper chest. Fast and shallow.

Did I want to go to the toilet again?

I needed a drink, but my dry mouth wouldn't even absorb a tiny bit of the water. It felt like I was pouring water over dry concrete.

This was it.

Let's go.

I followed the staff member, walking down the corridor towards the arena and waiting at the entrance.

My walkout music started, and this feeling was something different I recognised things change as my body and mind became one. Fear and excitement I saw were indeed one and the same. Walking out to a crowd and feeling their energy, the irreplaceable buzz in the venue, I soaked up every moment.

They were here to see me show off my skills.

I could get used to this limelight, I thought.

Then I saw my opponent.

He was terrifying.

He was and still is a beast of a man.

A Scotsman with more muscles than I have ever seen and the meanest-looking face. He looked like he'd been chewing wasps, and he looked at me as though I had put them in his mouth.

He was truly a physical specimen and stood across from me, ready to punch a hole through my head. As we faced each other in the arena, the referee motioned the beginning of the fight.

My opponent powered toward me at a terrifying pace, and the strangest thing happened.

Everything went quiet.

Time slowed down.

I couldn't hear the crowd any longer, just my inner dialogue as a voice spoke to me: "If you kick him in the head right now, you'll knock him out. His left hand is low. Do it."

So I lifted my right leg high into the air, and my foot and shin collided with the side of his face with an almighty thud.

Then, my opponent was falling to the floor, unconscious.

Three seconds, and it was all over. I was victorious and the owner of the fastest knockout the sport had ever seen. My first foray into professional combat was a successful one and one of many that provided me with great experience and stories to teach others. I also received a trophy and, more importantly, made a genuinely close friend that day, too, in my opponent. I was lucky it went the way it did on the night.

More interesting and rewarding than anything, though, was the feeling I'd received after the bout, which is one not many fighters or competitors ever really mention or talk about.

Relief.

Sweet relief that it is all over.

That the pressure can abate. That all of those envisioned outcomes are irrelevant. That the stress and worry is over.

Thirty minutes ago, back in the changing rooms, as I was readying up to fight, I told myself "you're not doing this again. This is definitely the last time."

I didn't think I could handle another one like that again.

But . . . maybe just one more time.

We have all had this experience in one way or another in our life.

I was terrified of putting myself out there.

In hindsight, I'm so glad I pushed through the fear. How have you pushed through in the past? How will you push through in the future?

Being vulnerable and stepping on the stage to compete scared me massively, but had I not done it, I wouldn't be the coach I am, the man I am, and I wouldn't have been able to write this book.

Professor Joseph Campbell once said, "The cave you fear to enter holds the treasure you seek."

By the end of this book, you will realise that if you want to achieve lofty goals and live the life of your dreams, you need to enter those caves you're most hesitant to approach. They hold the key to reaching the path that you are destined to travel.

CHAPTER 2
NO NEWS LIKE BAD NEWS

"Nothing travels faster than the speed of light with the possible exception of bad news, which obeys its own special laws."

Douglas Adams

I realised I had a choice.

In 2008, I made an active choice that, with the help of hindsight, was instrumental in me living the life I desired. More importantly, it also provided me with the opportunity to live happily and free of fear.

My choice: I could listen daily to strangers and their biased opinions about events around the world from a fixed perspective. I could choose to read gossip about many people, mostly those I didn't know, had never met, or who had no influence over my life. I could hear how people, who were revered and thought of as the greatest only weeks or months ago, suddenly aren't good enough anymore or capable at whatever they're currently doing.

Athletes, actors, performers, artists, politicians: the list was endless. Given enough time, it seemed they would all eventually become targets. I witnessed those aiming high, risking it all for a dream, being criticised by those in the cheapest seats.

I could watch and learn daily. I could receive minute-by-minute updates on death, famine, devastation, destruction, pain, horror, sadness, and deceit from around the world. I could learn about the many negative character traits of influential people and those in power. A cursory glance at such a list would make anyone wonder who would want to consume this kind of material daily and for what purpose.

But when you realise it's the mainstream media, you understand how we all get pulled into the negative thinking trap. It becomes ingrained in our culture. When I recognised that what I fed my mind - what I read, watched, and listened to - directly influenced my outlook on life and how I lived, I made a pivotal decision.

I stopped being a consumer of the mainstream media. The TV news was turned off. Newspapers remained untouched. Radios were silenced. News notifications were disabled. They sell fear, and it's big business, and we consume it often unknowingly.

There can be no argument against the media's instrumental role in instilling fearful thoughts, pushing them onto their consumers and the general public alike. Images of people dying in the street due to a virus that resulted in lockdowns were everywhere.

They sell us fear; we don't recognise it as we absorb it. This constant barrage impacts our subconscious beliefs and thoughts. All this fear keeps us in a perpetual low state, second-guessing every decision and action. Paralysed by anticipated negative outcomes, we often choose never to start for fear of failure or imagined regrets.

The media's grip was most evident from the start of the 2020 pandemic, presenting images of people dropping dead in China, mass burial grounds being prepared, and hospitals being overrun. Instructions were often contradictory: wash your hands while singing 'Happy Birthday,' wear masks in some situations but not others, and maintain distance from everyone. The majority complied, fueled by fear and confusion.

While many of the guidelines during the pandemic made sense given the information available, the concern lies in the presentation of the information.

Fear and drama weren't just critical to our news channels during the pandemic. It has always been the way.

I remember when I was young, and the news at ten would come on the TV. The intro was all about being dramatic and getting the audience on tenterhooks.

The loud chime of Big Ben.

Then: "On today's news," reads the presenter.

Bong!!! Follows the dramatic loud bell toll.

"The War on Terror."

Bong!!!

"Hospitals Overburdened."

Bong!!!

"Death in the Streets."

Fear and drama have always been staples of our news channels. But it's not just the news and media that contribute to our collective anxieties. Daytime shows, reality TV, and our social media feeds all play a part. This constant exposure can leave us feeling down, envious, and inadequate.

Reality TV shows reveal certain negative traits from people that make us doubt our relationships and resolve. We see others gossiping and judging from afar, causing us to judge, too. Unknowingly our judgement then just bounces back on to us.

The Bible speaks multiple times about the judgement of others. How we are quick to pass blame and to point to others' flaws without first attending to and noticing our own shortcomings.

"How can you say to your brother, 'Brother, let me take the speck out of your eye when you yourself fail to see the plank in your own eye?

You hypocrite, first take the plank out of your eye, and then you will see clearly to remove the speck from your brother's eye."
Matthew 7:3-5

That judgment causes us lots of pain and suffering. I have found that most would rather judge others than turn our gaze inward on ourselves. Instead of casting that first stone, what if we all looked inside first and practiced reflection, instead of blame?

When we judge or partake in gossip, it not only leaves us with a deep-seated guilty feeling—it creates doubt about ourselves and makes us believe others gossip about us, too.

This is a short ride to worrying to much about the opinions of others. When we're too mindful of others' thoughts about us, instead of being open to our possibility and honest with our notions of who we are and what we're meant to do, we become fearful.

We pretend to be someone we aren't in order to impress others. We live in fear, in shame, in silence, and walk forward repressing our self. To be Fearless by Design is to embrace who we are with conviction.

It tells us more still in the Bible. The judgement of others, ignoring forgiveness and understanding, only leaves us in pain, in suffering, and in judgement.

"Do not judge, or you too will be judged. For in the same 'way you judge others, you will be judged, and with the measure you use, it will be measured to you."

Matthew 7:1-5

When I first talked about avoiding the news, many asked how I could keep up with current affairs. Modern society often equates staying updated with intelligence. But with instant communication tools, traditional news sources have become somewhat redundant. Eliminating these sources, one realises their minimal impact on day-to-day life.

Programs like "Big Brother," "Love Island," and others showcase the plethora of negative behaviours we're capable of, amplified in short, dramatic segments. They subconsciously lower our state of mind to a place of fear, doubt, and comparison, due to the behaviours and actions we see on the screen. When you take twenty-four-hour long days and whittle them down to forty-five minute shows stuffed with dramatised clips of negative, headline-grabbing behaviours, nothing good can happen.

Our social media feeds are much the same when we aren't consciously aware of their adverse effects. If you're in touch with your emotions and how you feel, you'll notice that spending an extended period on social media can leave you feeling sluggish, low, envious, and rather flat.

Seeing the "best moments" of people's lives—and by "'best," I mean those supposedly perfect moments that likely took hours to set up to appear spontaneous - still places us in a negative state. We can feel utterly inadequate when we see what others possess, who they're with, and what they're doing, all the while feeling helpless and lacklustre in our endeavours and achievements.

When we observe others on social media, we often experience what's known as FOMO—fear of missing out. This feeling can drive us to engage in activities we don't genuinely enjoy. We might buy things we don't need or even truly want, simply out of fear of being left behind or missing out. It compels us to visit places we'd rather not, with people we don't particularly like, doing things we'd rather avoid, all because of this pervasive fear of missing out.

In my coaching role, the topic of nightlife often arises when people recount their younger days. The number of individuals who claimed to enjoy those club nights is staggering. They feigned enjoyment of the loud music, the late hours, the alcohol, and the culture, not because it resonated with their personalities, but because it was the expected thing to do. They feared the loss of friendships if they opted out.

As we grow older, many of us develop the capacity to say 'no' when we feel it's appropriate. Possessing the strength and conviction to decline is incredibly empowering, and when used wisely, can be incredibly liberating. If you have aspirations and are influenced by FOMO, here's a piece of advice: if you're saying "yes" to one thing, consider what you might be saying "no" to as a result.

CHAPTER 3
FIGHT, FLIGHT, AND FREEZE

"I'm not afraid of death. I just don't want to be there when it happens."

Woody Allen

Have you ever watched your cat or dog just as they sense a knock on the door and a visitor is approaching? Some panic before the door is knocked on or the doorbell has rung and hurry off as fast as you've seen them move. Others behave the exact opposite: they charge to the door and stand steadfast, ready to protect their property and all that's within it to the death. In a nutshell, that's fight or flight.

But what about freeze?

Freeze is where we get the saying, 'Like a deer frozen in the headlights.' When a creature is in the middle of the road and a car is hurtling towards it, it stays stuck to the spot through sheer fear and indecision until the inevitable crash happens.

Fight or flight is the term given to the physiological responses that all humans, and most animals, experience under duress, occurring when the sympathetic branch of the nervous system is triggered.

Our bodies operate using the Autonomic Nervous System, or ANS for short. Our ANS has two branches: the parasympathetic, known as the rest and digest branch, and the sympathetic, referred to as fight or flight. This response would have been paramount for survival when we were hunter-gatherers, living wild and hunting for our food regularly with the threat of attack possible at any time.

When we enter this state, our bodies adapt to help us fight or flee from an aggressor.

Our pupils dilate, allowing us to detect threats more intently on the horizon or the prey we wish to hunt.

We get dry mouths because our saliva production is inhibited.

Our heart rates surge, pumping blood to our vital muscles, aiding us as we wrestle and fight to the death or sprint away for our lives.

More blood rushes to our heart and lungs, pumping oxygen throughout our bodies as our airways expand.

Our livers release more glycogen to convert to glucose, fueling our muscles.

This state stimulates the release of epinephrine, known as adrenaline, which helps transmit nerve signals to muscles and instructs our bodies to stay alert until danger passes.

The blood supply to our stomach is reduced, and the vessels aiding digestion constrict, as our bodies determine that these are not needed, prioritising oxygen-rich blood for our brains and skeletal muscles that is crucial for survival. Our brains also ramp up, enabling us to make swift, intuitive decisions about threats or possible escape routes.

It's safe to say that when my first opponent walked into the ring, that hulking Scotsman with more muscles than I'd ever seen and a face that looked like he'd been chewing wasps, my sympathetic nervous system was on fire.

When we harness this system correctly in the right environment, it serves us immensely. Who hasn't heard tales of a mother demonstrating astonishing feats of strength and determination? Lifting heavy obstacles that have fallen on their child or block their path? Such stories of physical defiance are commonplace when our nervous system deploys its tools as intended, seemingly removing our self-imposed limitations.

The sympathetic state (fight or flight) should only be active for a short, designated period. In this context, it fulfils its role perfectly. But if we remain in this state for an extended duration, it can be harmful. Some suggest that as hunters, we could exploit this knowledge. Some even theorise that humans might have practised persistence hunting, tracking animals for hours or days until they succumbed to fatigue and heat exhaustion. The adrenaline of being pursued exacts a toll, not just physically but mentally.

The constant stress and fear induced by the predator in their prey, keeping them in a perpetual fight or flight state, bear many similarities to modern humans. The stresses and stressors of contemporary life can feel unending.

Bills to pay.

Being a good parent.

Staying fit, losing weight, and remaining healthy.

Being a loving spouse.

Maintaining a home.

Earning a sufficient income.

Feeling adequate.

Battling self-doubt.

Grappling with self-worth.

Any of that sound familiar to you, too?

Financial struggles and anticipated negative outcomes, while different from wild threats, still register as tangible threats and trigger the same physiological reactions. Our minds are creative machines. They excel at conjuring images and stories that feel very real. These perceived threats, even if from imagined scenarios, elicit the same changes in the body as actual threats, even if there's no real danger to us, no hulking Scotsman looming, no lion on our tail, no fear of actual bankruptcy right over the horizon.

The power of overthinking and the problem of allowing our anxieties to derail us from our best selves and possible futures is everywhere in life. So, how do we fight back against it and gain the inner control, calm, and fortitude we need to preserve?

A LONG TRAIN RIDE

Many years ago, my sensei told me an old tale about two bare-knuckle street fighters.

These two fighters were the best of the best and the toughest, meanest back-street brawlers around.

One of them, from London, was undefeated in all of his fights. He was the king of the streets and felled everyone he faced in brutal and devastating fashion.

The damage he'd caused to his opponents in previous fights was legendary. Fighters had their noses, cheekbones and jaws broken when fighting him. In one match, an opponent even had his eye fall out of the socket due to the ferocity of the champ's punches.

The other fighter was from up North and was no less skilled than the champion from the South.

Tales also echoed about this new challenger. His evasiveness and skillset were unmatched by any previous opponent the southern champion had faced.

When word got out about this fight, many were excited to see the champion face what they thought would be a true test. The date was set. The talk began to swirl.

The Northern fighter's friends heard about the match and who their friend would be facing. They knew of his ferocity. They repeated the tales of brutality and meanness they had heard, many third-, fourth-, and fifth-hand. They pled for the

Northern warrior not to go, implored that this was the one man he shouldn't fight.

With their fears projected onto him, they were speaking with what they thought was love.

The Northern champion, unaware that all this worry was soaking deeply into his subconscious, simply he told his friends all would be okay.

On a cold Winter morning, in the early hours, the northern champion kissed his wife and child farewell and headed toward the train station to travel to the fight.

He was a little sleepy. He hadn't slept the best last night. He'd been tossing and turning. His thoughts ran away, imagining fight outcomes that overpowered his ability to stay calm and sleep.

So he reassured himself he'd have a sleep and rest on the train.

When he got to his seat, he tried to relax and tried to sleep. But he couldn't switch the worry off.

Try as he might, thoughts of his opponent dominated his mind. At every station he passed, and with every stop the train made to pick up and drop off passengers, he felt the adrenaline in his gut. Dripping like a tap. Echoing. Growing as he got closer.

He thought back to what his friends had said about this man he would be facing.

Would he end up hurt and damaged like so many of the rest before him?

Defeated and broken?

The fear of losing consumed him as he continued his train journey, moving closer and closer to the battleground, closer to hostility, close to danger, to injury, to failure . . . and further away from *safety*.

As he went through Newcastle, his mind filled with visions of his opponent.

At Manchester, he thought, *What if he hits me like when that guy lost his eye?*

As Stafford went by, he couldn't stop thinking about losing.

And as he approached Birmingham, he thought, *What if he beats me?*

When the train pulled into London, the fight promoters were there to greet the Northern fighter as he exited.

They waited, ready to welcome the warrior and take him to the fight. Then they waited a while longer, but there was still no sign of this formidable warrior.

All the passengers had left the train now, but their man hadn't appeared yet. So they went to help him, boarding the train, thinking maybe he was having issues with his luggage.

As they get to the fighter's seat, the fighter was nowhere anywhere to be seen. On second glance, the promoters saw a note.

It said.

To the champ,
I'm sorry.

You beat me in Birmingham.

THE POWER OF THE MIND'S EYE

Comedian Jerry Seinfeld once said, "According to most studies, people's number one fear is public speaking. Number two is death. Death is number two. Does that sound right? This means that to the average person, if you go to a funeral, you're better off in the casket than doing the eulogy."

Take a minute and visualise that you've been called up to do a public speaking event. Imagine it's happening right now and in a short while, you'll be stepping up to take centre stage in front of a hundred people. Some of these faces are familiar, a few are work colleagues, while many are complete strangers.

Backstage, you catch glimpses of the audience through a slight crack in the door, all of them waiting, anticipating your talk and eager to hear what you have to share. The MC finally announces your name, and after an elaborate introduction, you make your way to centre stage amidst applause. You pause, awaiting the hush after your entrance, and it feels like you've been standing there an eternity.

Now, it's time to gather your thoughts for the hour-long talk ahead. Scanning the room, you see a variety of expressions. While some seem keenly interested, others appear indifferent, and a few even seem mildly irritated that you've dared to step up and speak—or at least, that's the impression you get. Immerse yourself in this imagined scenario and spend a moment visualising this scene in detail.

Can you feel those familiar nerves beginning to stir?

For many, the mere thought of public speaking—a fear said to rank even above death, remember—can be profoundly unsettling.

VISUALISATION: WHERE WE WIN OR LOSE

As you will discover throughout this book, our imaginations, specifically how we visualise situations, are extremely powerful. They can create and cause outcomes, and sometimes those outcomes are not the ones we need.

Looking back to our tale about the fighter on the train, each visualisation the Northern fighter manifested took him one step closer to defeat.

Every station created more disempowering thoughts that lead to and created more feelings of helplessness.

If we are unable to see a way out, or to see a way to victory, we will struggle to put up a fight.

We must develop and utilise coping mechanisms like breathwork and meditation to help us to move onward, shifting our ANS from a sympathetic (fight or flight) response, to a parasympathetic (rest and digest) response; a place of confident peace and ease.

The parasympathetic state is intended as our predominant physiological state. It is us at our baseline, us as we are resting, and especially as we eat.

The term rest and digest comes from the body prioritising blood flow to the stomach, assisting in transporting nutrients to the blood and muscles that it absorbs from the food we eat.

Our heartbeat slows. We breathe at a slower, steadier pace. We can see paths through fear towards success, and victory.

Consider a deer in the wild. When hunted, their fight-or-flight response dumps adrenaline through their body. They burn off the adrenaline, flee from their predator, and then can continue in their parasympathetic state, resting, eating, recovering, and digesting.

The parasympathetic state is paramount for the health of the wild animal.

However, for modern man, sometimes we aren't afforded that luxury.

CHAPTER 4
STRESS ENVIRONMENTS

"Stress should be a powerful driving force, not an obstacle."

Bill Phillips

As a society, it seems a cultural norm to be exposed to continual stress daily.

Constant deadlines from our jobs and workplace. Fears of meeting bills and making payments on time. Mounting debt, parenting, being a good partner, and so the list goes on. Sometimes, causing us to feel that these stressors are never-ending.

If left unchecked over time and through not employing correct coping mechanisms, these fears can become chronic stress, causing a multitude of illnesses, ailments and health issues and concerns.

When we observe the sympathetic nervous system in use as it is intended, in an environment conducive to movement, one where we are given the opportunity to utilise and embrace the added physiological benefits and adaptations afforded to us from the hormonal changes, we then see states return to a calmer state—that of the parasympathetic or rest and digest.

The attacker or threat has been dealt with or removed, and our bodies have utilised all the excess adrenaline to its advantage, allowing us to calm down and return to a more relaxed state.

In the wild, we see this response from animals. They graze, see a disturbance, panic, respond, and escape. The fleeing from a predator or disturbance, checking again for safety, then a little 'shake off' with muscle twitches and then back to grazing.

However, in our working lives, the stress continues unabated for many. The sympathetic nervous system remains active as one stress replaces another.

The continuous, slow drip of adrenaline ceases to stop. And like a steady drip on a stone, it causes slow and steady damage to our physical and mental well-being.

It is relentless and unforgiving.

The damage being done can be difficult to prevent. As we are unable and incapable of clearing these hormones through use, as there is no immediate threat, we must address them directly. Many times, it isn't even a physical threat at all. Usually, a man-made concern like a bill or deadline, with an imagined undesired outcome that imprisons us in this awful state.

This can then lead us to lots of ailments and illnesses due to this stress.

In response to stress, our bodies release a hormone called cortisol.

Released from the adrenal glands that sit just above our kidneys, its role is pivotal in our fight-or-flight response.

We have cortisol receptors in most cells of our body, and when our bodies utilise it correctly, the hormone helps keep inflammation down, regulate blood pressure, and provide the proper physical and mental boost when needed.

When cortisol is raised, however, it can alter and shut down important functions within our bodies, leading to illness. After a physical threat has passed, all of our bodily functions should normalise, and we should return to the parasympathetic state of calm.

But if those fears, stressors and worries are real or imagined, constant and unforgiving, then we can struggle to return to our natural baseline resting state.

This can then lead to a plethora of health issues and concerns.

Anxiety, depression, heart disease, sleep issues, gut problems and autoimmunity are just a small amount of the problems we face when our bodies start improperly using these hormones.

Have you ever been stressed or anxious over an upcoming event, competition, or meeting that you've been visualising? You're trying to do your best to imagine the outcome you want.

During this process of worry, have you ever noticed that you're not hungry? Have you missed meals and left half-eaten plates of food?

This is due to cortisol shutting down your digestive system as it pulls all the needed attention away from your gut to help cope with this current threat . . . the one that isn't actually there.

It gets worse.

With your body's direct focus on the perceived threat, it decides to lower your immune system function, diverting resources elsewhere, as its concern isn't a cold or flu right now, but whatever is the immediate threat.

Suddenly we're not just worried and nutrient-deprived from unregistered hunger. We're ill, too.

In a similar fashion, surgeons utilise corticosteroids in organ transplant surgery to inhibit the body's immune response and prevent the rejection of the transplanted organ. In this situation, the practice is doing good and serving.

For us in daily life, the result is almost always the opposite.

ANXIETY

Anxiety can be defined as feelings of worry, nervousness, or unease about something with an uncertain outcome.

In today's society, it seems many are living their lives in an anxious state. The media that we're bombarded by can worsen this state. As can our own mentality, where we are beset by what ifs, worries, and worst-case outcomes, much like our Northern warrior felled by his own thoughts on that long train ride.

Our fears appear in our minds, manifest in our lives, and affect our bodies.

It can become very easy to allow anxieties to take over our visualisation space and steal our comfort. Anxiety dwells in the future, in the worrying about outcomes. It thrives on our thoughts about events that are yet to happen.

It is even easier to fall victim to anxiety when we are subjected to or allow ourselves to watch and listen to negative influences, whether it's mainstream media, or a group of well-meaning friends who are telling us how we'll fail to achieve a goal or dream.

How many days have you wasted imagining meetings, encounters, or outcomes versus living in the moment? Visualising exactly how an interaction or altercation will take place and then the day or moment arrives, and it goes nothing like we had sat fretting about.

It happens to us all. But we can all learn to protect against this trap as well.

"Our anxiety does not empty tomorrow of its sorrows, but only empties today of its strengths."

C.H Spurgeon

VISUALISATION REALIZED

Your armour against anxiety? You might have guessed it: visualisation.

In 1996, Psychologist Alan Richardson performed a study at the University of Chicago to test results on the efficacy of visualisation. The results were astounding.

Dr. Alan Richardson collected a group of randomly selected students and asked them to take a series of free throws at a basketball hoop.

Dr. Richardson's team made a note of all the scores and how each individual performed at throwing the ball into the basket on their first tries.

After all the students had thrown the basketball and had their results recorded, the research team divided the participants into three separate groups.

The three groups were appointed strict criteria to follow with their practice and were asked to maintain and perform their assigned task for thirty days.

The three groups were:

Group One

This group were forbidden from basketball practice of any kind. They were not allowed to throw a ball for the next thirty days.

Group Two

This second group had to practice their free throws for thirty minutes daily for the thirty days— consistent and purposeful practice.

Group Three

The third group were allowed to come to the gym, but they were forbidden from touching a basketball. For thirty minutes a day they had to sit and visualise throwing the ball, and the ball landing in the basket successfully every throw.

After the thirty days had passed, all of the students were required to return to the hall and take the same number of free throws that they had at the start of the study.

Here's what the results showed :

Group One

Those who didn't practice any basketball or think about it for the last thirty days showed zero improvement.

Group Two

The group that had been on the court, physically practising daily, showed a massive twenty-four percent improvement in their original scores through consistent practice.

Group Three

Those from group three who weren't allowed to actively practice on the court or to touch a basketball but were told only to visualise their successful shots improved by an amazing twenty-three percent.

A one percent difference!

Only a one percent difference between groups two and three. That shows just how influential our minds can be over our physical bodies.

This study also shows how powerful a tool visualising can be, not just for athletes but for everybody who wants to improve their skills, in any area of their life.

If you're a keen golfer looking to improve your skills on the green, then how about embracing these visualisation techniques to help improve your swing without needing to be out the house or office. Visualise yourself, club in hand, and imagine the movements through your body, those you would perform whilst actually swinging the club.

See the fairway, let your body relax into its stance (in your mind) as you make the mind body connection, pull the club back and release, hearing the noise the club makes as it hits the ball perfectly. The more details you can put in to this visualisation, the better the outcome will be.

This technique has also been embraced by athletes that like to lift weights. Through visualising their muscles being used to lift weights as they were resting, imagining themselves doing their favourite strength exercises caused them to increase their lifts by up to fifteen percent. You could easily do the same. In combination of your regular gym visits and weightlifting, why not add in some visualisation sessions to assist in your strength and muscle gains?

Visualisation is a tremendously powerful skill. The downside? Oftentimes we use it incorrectly, and what we visualise (outcomes other than those we really desire) makes us feel overwhelmed and even more anxious.

We lie in bed at night and imagine the worst-case outcomes. We place ourselves in the fight or flight state and cause feelings of nausea and a high heart rate. With zero opportunity to utilise the benefit of the hormones, visualisation becomes a terrible hindrance.

It's important to remember that neither the sympathetic nor parasympathetic state is good or bad.

They work excellently for their designated purpose. They both serve accordingly for when the time suits. I'm sure that if we were in a life-threatening altercation, we would want to be engaged in a fight-or-flight response, not thinking about taking a nap or what we are going to eat.

It's what we bring to the equation with our mindsets and patterns of thought that colour these physiological states, for better or worse.

We are so good at imagining and creating these scenarios in our minds—both the things we do and *don't* want to happen. Sometimes we don't even realise how much damage we are causing to ourselves with these thoughts.

Things gradually take their toll without us noticing.

Habits can form without realisation.

We gain extra weight from slowly easing off our healthy eating plan. The one single cigarette with a drink that turns into a pack and multiple drinks a night.

Usually, we don't spot the damage done until it's too late.

Putting three or four pounds of weight on over a year seems insignificant, but over a decade, that's a significant shift in body weight that could have adverse health results.

Our stress levels face a similar bombardment.

Visualising our way into *more* stress continually causes damage to our physiological health through these imagined outcomes and responses.

This is why our environments are so important to our mental well-being and development. If we are continuously around drama, pain, conflict, upset, and aggression, no matter the source, we accept it as normal. In turn, we begin to easily visualise it, which just reinforces those experiences happening.

TV shows, dramas, and reality TV, as I mentioned in chapter two, can take a similar psychological toll, which then takes a physiological toll, without us even realising it. They are manufactured to manipulate and play on our stress responses to keep us on the hook for more.

As a former mixed martial arts fighter, anxiety became a regular occurrence in my life like it does for many of us under high pressure. I was constantly worrying about the outcome of a fight.

If I won, how I won, and how instrumental that win would be to my career would all play havoc with my mind and thoughts. Until I developed the tools to deal with it and use it to my advantage.

We've started to better understand those tools (mainly how our ANS functions and how we can manage our thoughts by proper visualisation practices). But let's get deeper into concrete techniques to manage our collective anxiety by first looking deeper at how anxiety, or fear to be more specific, affects those of us in high-pressure environments.

CHAPTER 5
THE FEAR OF FAILURE

"There is only one thing that makes a dream impossible to achieve: the fear of failure."

Paulo Coelho

Whether the environment is a cage, a stage, an office, or a ring; whether you're a high-flying business exec or entrepreneur; or whether you're as far from an athlete as you can imagine— understanding how fear works and limits us can help us, no matter our professions or passions.

As a fighter, my fear of being physically hurt in competition was minimal. Strange as it sounds, it's not really something fighters think about.

You would think that facing another fighter who has trained to win and whose sole intention is to hurt you and make you quit would cause some concern for your own health and safety. But no fighters ever mention it.

Personally, I suffered many devastating injuries during my career. Some of which, unfortunately, cut my career short way too soon. But most of these were done through training and overuse, not usually whilst in active competition.

In all my years of coaching amateur first-timers to world champions, I've never once had an athlete mention being afraid of being hit or hurt.

As the saying goes: "If you're gonna go swimming, you're gonna get wet."

The thought of being hurt never bothered me, but there was one thing that did keep me up at night. And it's the one thing that keeps so many high performers up at night, too: Losing.

Or more accurately, the fear of losing, which is at its heart the fear of failure.

SIDESTEPPING FEAR OF FAILURE THROUGH WHITE-BELT THINKING

How many dreams and goals have never even started due to a fear of failure? Have you ever been so fearful of making a mistake that you didn't even dare to start something?

There's a phrase I use in my coaching practices that applies across all of life's endeavours and removes the panic and fear from our minds when it is utilised correctly and as intended.

Competence breeds confidence.

When we're not confident at a task, it usually means we are inexperienced or not knowledgeable enough on a subject. Confidence comes from the commitment to learn a skill and all its involved elements.

The great Stoic philosopher Epictetus said, "*If you wish to improve, be content to appear foolish or clueless in extraneous matters.*"

Epictetus is talking about the concept of beginner's mind, being open to making mistakes, to learning through doing. Being a beginner is normal. At one point in life, we are all beginners at just about everything we do. Yet our ego feels the need to protect its identity; it attempts to keep its worth by desperately not wanting to appear to be a beginner.

In martial arts, we call beginner's mind the white-belt mentality, that constant belief that there are always so many things to learn and experience. Removing the ego in these matters makes learning much more fun and infinitely more fruitful.

"It is impossible for a man to learn what he thinks he already knows."

Epictetus

When we have adopted the ego-driven, fear-based mindset, it becomes very difficult to learn anything. We close ourselves off to so many new lessons, new experiences, and new people. We limit our expansion and capability. We're so riddled by our ego's fear of judgement and failure, that we often never even start.

Furthermore, we create even more limiting self-talk to reinforce our choice to not do something and attempt to make ourselves look less foolish to protect ourselves.

When the occasion has arisen to do something you've daydreamed or fantasised about, how often have you talked yourself out of seizing that opportunity?

Do any of the following sound familiar?

"I'm too old."

"I'm too young."

"I'm too thin."

"I'm too fat."

"I don't know how to."

"I can't, I'm too small."

"I can't, I'm too big."

We're good at convincing ourselves we're right where we want to be (even when we're not) because it keeps us and our egos protected.

These self-limiting beliefs are the ultimate in protecting our egos and ensuring we will never fail.

Ever.

Because they won't even let us get started.

If I don't try, I can't get embarrassed; I can't lose; I can't fail.

SELF-LIMITING BELIEFS

Are you guilty of this defeatist self-talk? Is someone you love? I know I have been at times.

When I was younger, I often had these self-defeating thoughts at many different places and stages of my life. Back then, I thought it was just me.

Now, after coaching so many people and having the blessed opportunity to help people through tough times to help realise their potential, I know this talk is prevalent throughout society.

How many opportunities have you lost through giving power to these thoughts?

How many friendships could have been made if you hadn't played it safe?

What about love?

Maybe you ran from your true love?

What if your soul mate was destined to meet you that day, but you let fear control and restrain you, caving to that worry of looking foolish in front of people you didn't even know and who wouldn't even give you a second thought?

How we speak to ourselves is integral to living a happy and productive life.

Self-limiting beliefs are thoughts about ourselves that negatively impact us and prevent us from reaching our full potential.

We may be blissfully unaware of them until they are exposed and rooted out, but we pick many of them up in our early formative years and usually from those we love, like our parents, grandparents, siblings, and teachers.

Imagine a young boy with friends who play and love rugby.

The boy thinks he'd like to have a go at that and see if he enjoys it and could join the team.

Understandably, he's a little fearful, but he sees his friends doing it. So, why can't he?

So he mentions to his mum about training with the rugby team and seeing how he gets on.

"Mum, all my friends are playing rugby for the local team, and I think I'd like to give it a go. It seems like fun."

"Rugby?" His mum replies with a dubious, doubting tone in her question.

"Yes, mum, they train twice a week and then a game on Sundays."

"You're way too small for rugby."

He thinks to himself, *Am I too small?*

"You would hate it, too. You don't even like exercise."

Do I not like exercise? He ponders.

"You can't stick to training three times a week. You've not got the discipline. You'll want to quit."

Oh, maybe it's not for me then, he thinks. If I am small, unfit and dislike exercise, and I am a quitter, then it mustn't be for me. And my mum would know about me. She's my mum. She knows everything!

Our minds are akin to the most amazing fertile garden with the most nutritious soil.

But now the negative seeds are planted for the boy. With a little more negative energy and a little more fear, imagine how big these little seeds could grow over time.

We can plant the most beautiful of flowers, trees and bushes and take care of them daily. We can water and feed them and talk lovingly to them. Let them feel the breeze and the winds pushing against them so they can face adversity and grow stronger as they brace against difficulties. The garden could be beautiful and attract fascinating new wildlife and insects to help it grow and expand its horizons.

Or we could neglect this fertile ground and let it become overgrown with weeds and thorns that we overfeed. Suddenly the sunlight being blocked out due to the overgrown garden, putting everything in the shade. We can still talk to our plants, but instead of talking to them positively and telling them how wonderful they are and how they enrich our lives, we berate them and tell them how awful they are and how pathetic they look.

I doubt we would get many visitors to our closed-off garden. Not many creatures would want to come.

I don't think there's a choice as to which garden we would prefer to own and sit in. But how many of us have, in our lives, chosen to cultivate the garden of misery, low self-worth, and limiting beliefs?

All the weeds feed an abundance of negativity, gossip and anxiety. And the only visitors to this garden are fear, selfishness, and ego, keeping itself secure in the darkness and shadows.

If we were to take mindful care of our garden, though, removing the weeds, those negative self-beliefs and thoughts, and carefully replacing them with new plants, positive affirmations, and beliefs about ourselves, gradually, with the correct care and attention, our garden could change to a beautiful plot brimming with the most wonderful plants and wildlife.

We don't just pick up these fearful, limiting beliefs from our loved ones. We can also develop them from fear in response to a painful experience or past trauma.

How often were you embarrassed as a child and vowed never to be put in that situation again?

Like when your teacher asked a question, only for you to give the wrong answer in front of the class?

The teacher might have berated you for not knowing, or the whole classroom of pupils might have laughed out loud at your inability to recall the answer. From that moment on a seed of shame, which has its roots in fear as well as embarrassment, was planted.

The fear of making a mistake.

The fear of appearing foolish.

Regardless of the origins of your negative self-talk, be mindful of its experience and its potential power to limit you. When you notice the negative talk, as inconspicuous and small as it may seem, pause for reflection. Slowly, over time, replace it with a positive thought about yourself

The importance of self-talk isn't just crucial for our mental health and our ability to cope with and try new experiences; it also has a massive effect on our physical cells at the deepest level, as we'll explore in depth in a later chapter.

Biologist Bruce Lipton talks in length about this and likens our self-talk to that of a Dictaphone or voice recorder. When we speak negatively and notice ourselves doing it, we must rewind and record over the negative belief with a positive one.

As we pause for reflection on the negative, change the thought to a positive one and then keep thinking of that positive, uplifting, empowering thought in its place until it eradicates the original negative thought.

It is important to remember that our inner dialogue is not just idle chatter but a transformative force that can dictate the direction of our lives. In embracing positive self-talk, as authors Bruce Lipton and Dr. Joseph Murphy speak of, we can steer ourselves to a much happier and fulfilling existence.

STAY IN YOUR LANE

"Who does she think she is?"

How often have you heard that said about someone trying to achieve something out of their comfort zone?

Have *you* ever thought it?

Sometimes when we see people exuding confidence, we rush to judge them. They're willing to put themselves forward, to put themselves in the limelight and try new things, looking for new experiences openly. Yet they get judged by the fearful.

When we spend our lifetime judging others, we don't realise that in reality, we are just judging ourselves.

As we think of ourselves joining in a different activity, risking it all on a business idea or move, writing that screenplay, making that movie, going back to school, whatever it may be, we imagine the gossip about us.

What will people think?

We can visualise them talking about us negatively, saying, "Just who do you think you are?"

Each thought and vision makes us feel more and more doubtful about our decisions.

Through Jiu-jitsu and martial arts, I have found tremendous pleasure in helping many people not only get in the best physical shape of their lives but in their best mental condition, too. As they face adversity and physical exertion, pushing ahead while taking the challenges as they come, their confidence and self-talk continually improves.

I have so many members at our academy who put off training at all because of fear of judgement, failure, and what others may say or think. They are beset by thoughts like:

"Am I too old?'"

"I am too overweight. I am going to have to get fitter first."

"Am I too weak?"

"People like me don't do martial arts."

Here they are looking to make a positive life change like starting a new martial art like Jiu-jitsu, and yet they stop themselves because of what others *might* think. Then there is the other, sneaky regret. I've seen it again and again. When someone finally does take up Jiu-jitsu, they almost always regret not having done it sooner. Don't let this be you. If there is something you feel you should be doing, go do it.

"Though you cannot go back
And make a brand new start, my friend
Anyone can start from now
And make a brand new end."

John Maxwell

THE TRIPLE FILTER TEST OF SOCRATES

There's an apocryphal tale credited to the wise philosopher Socrates.

One day, Socrates was approached by an acquaintance who asked in an excited tone, "Do you know what I just heard about one of your pupils?"

"Whoa," Socrates replied. "Slow down. Before you proceed to tell me this tale of my friend and student, I'd like to pass it through my triple filters test. First, is what you are about to tell me true? Are you certain of that?"

"Well, no. I have only just heard the news a moment ago."

"Ok," replied Socrates. "You are uncertain of the story's validity, but not to worry, let us see if it passes the second filter. Is what you're going to tell me about my pupil something good?"

"Absolutely not!" The man exclaimed. "It's actually . . . "

"So!" Socrates interrupted the man, "This thing you wish to tell me is not good, and you are uncertain if it is true, but let us see if it is useful."

"No, not at all," the man replied.

"So if what you're about to tell me is neither true, good nor useful, why say it at all?"

Most gossip is like this. It is based on fearful thinking, It wants to take the limelight off of someone else's success or to try to dim their light for fear that ours won't shine bright enough, when all it does is dull us all and cause us to stay in the shadows through fear of the light being pointed on us, on our mistakes, on our misgivings.

The fear of others' opinions is a massive obstacle to overcome on our way to freedom of living the life we want to. Caring about what others think will prevent you from living your best life.

As the saying goes, "Those who mind, don't matter, and those who matter, don't mind."

If you only knew just how little and infrequently others thought of you, then you wouldn't give going after your dreams a second thought.

So, if you're doing something that brings you joy and happiness, something you feel aligns with your purpose, then go ahead.

How many unique world-changing ideas have been buried and taken to the cemetery before they even had the chance to be called into being and put to use? Dreams that could have altered the way we live.

An artist creating inspiring pieces of art that motivate another young artist to do the same, inspiring thoughts and emotions in those who see it. Musicians not creating music from their hearts that could speak to millions. A director creating a thought-provoking movie. All for the fear of what others may think, all because someone may ask: "Who do they think they are?"

Know this, if you are holding something inside, back and deep down for this reason, for the sake of being afraid of failing and fearful of what the critics may say, you will regret it always and likely turn sour just like them. You will become like those making you feel like you can't achieve something.

Could you imagine an NBA superstar like Michael Jordan gossiping about someone who aimed higher, strived, and risked achieving more?

Me neither.

I think it's worth noting that those doing better than someone will not spend time to criticise. People don't judge down. Only to those who are doing what they won't, can't or, more than likely, would really like to but dare not through fear.

We often base many of our fears of failing on others' opinions. We care so much about their opinion, how they will view us, and what they all think that we freeze for fear of those mistakes, but we must remember that in every mistake, there is a lesson to be learned.

Remember how little "they" think of you and go ahead and do what you dream. Make all the mistakes needed along the way. Embrace the journey.

"Enter their minds, and you'll find the judges you're so afraid of and how judiciously they judge themselves"

Marcus Aurelius

CHAPTER 6
FEAR AND THE ATHLETE

"Never say never, because limits, like fears, are often just an illusion."

Michael Jordan

As a fighter, it would always happen in the weeks leading up to fight night. The voice would pop up.

"This fight you've got," it would say to me.

Then, I would be continuously thinking about the fight. My body automatically responding to the imagined stimulus.

How could it not?

It thought I was in a fight.

In my head, I was.

My body didn't know any different.

In the middle of my professional fight career, as I gained a lot of momentum in reaching the top spot for being the best heavyweight in Europe, I had amassed professional titles and accolades, and my skills and abilities were well known to those within the sport.

In one of my fights during that time, I fought an outstanding, extremely tough, solid fighter.

I fought many like that, but this one was a former rugby player turned MMA fighter. What he lacked in skill set, he made up for in desire, athleticism, and tenacity.

He was a great fighter, but without intending to sound arrogant, skillset-wise, he wasn't close to my technical knowledge and ability.

But he wanted that win. He wanted a fight. And he had self-confidence in the bucketloads, something, with hindsight, I realised I was starting to lack.

I remember the lead-up to the fight.

I had suffered massive issues with my neck, including immense pain and nerve damage that would later derail my whole career way too early.

But there were many lessons learned before, during, and after that fight as well.

Like all my losses had, it taught me the most significant lesson at precisely the right time. I just had to be ready to accept the lesson. My losses and failings didn't make me a loser or a failure, far from it, as I would later come to learn. I didn't realise it at the time, but the sleepless nights, the pressure on reaching a destination (the UFC or a big promotion), the need to win, how I'd tied my identity to being this great fighter, and a whole host of other issues that highly competitive athletes (and entrepreneurs) commonly face all led me to a deep exploration of performance anxiety, another form of anxiety that has its roots in fear of failure, and that undercuts so many of us from reaching our full potential.

PERFORMANCE ANXIETY

Unsurprisingly, being locked inside a cage fighting another man can be a daunting place to be. But as I said earlier, for a fighter, the daunting part isn't the idea of being hurt.

What does is are the thoughts related to our family, the promoters, the crowd, our sponsors, our mistakes, and how we will be perceived if we fail. This crosses over to any sport, too—football, rugby, boxing, tennis, and more.

It exists outside the world of sports as well. I'm sure it's present in your life, where and however you spend your days.

In my fight, for me to win, it just came down to doing what I was capable of.

Simple in theory.

But my fear of underperforming caused me to manifest this thing I really didn't want.

A loss.

Being a loser.

The self-made pressure, possibly strengthened by those around me, built up over the weeks before. This caused me to freeze when I didn't get the finish I had anticipated.

The one I had visualised.

I got in the cage and immediately wanted out as quickly as possible.

I hated it.

I loved martial arts and combat sports, but I wanted out at that moment of my life.

I'd regularly get the thought of, "This is the last time I do this," before many fights. I knew these thoughts would come and go. Normally as soon as I walked out to the crowd, thoughts like that would disappear or at the least be subdued, and I would aim to enjoy the experience. But this time was different.

I didn't look afraid or anxious to the casual observer because my exterior was as calm and stoic as usual. But on the inside, my heart was racing, and I was terrified.

I was like a duck in water.

Just like in my first pro fight, as I got in the cage with the former rugby player, I looked like that duck gliding across the surface of a pond. Graceful and calm, leaving a slight ripple through the sereneness of the water, while under the surface, their little legs were thrashing wildly. That was me. Again.

In the fight, I wrestled my opponent to the mat, and we hit the mat hard. My neck jarred heavily to the side, sending shockwaves down my back and, more worryingly, numbness down my arm.

Have I caused my spine and neck permanent damage by fighting? I thought. *Can I win this fight with one arm not working correctly?*

Panicked thoughts and unhelpful visualisations of a possible, grim future when I should have concentrated on the present moment and my opponent flooded over me.

This pain and self-talk exacerbated my panic and desire to get out as soon as possible. My imagination added more fuel to the fire as my arm refused to respond as it should.

The referee stood us back up to our feet, and again I initiated the wrestle and dragged my opponent back down to the mat as we grappled on the floor.

I managed to secure a triangle choke, a submission using my legs around my opponent's neck, squeezing the carotid artery, causing them to pass out from cutting off the blood supply to the brain if they didn't submit.

I've got him, I thought. ***This is tight.***

I carried on my squeeze, but I couldn't quite find the angle or seem to find the finish.

My legs just didn't have their usual strength or stamina.

My opponent started to work himself free from the strangle. I could slowly feel my legs fatiguing as he managed to escape the choke.

As the choke released, my opponent was over me as he rained down heavy blows continuously at my head.

They didn't hurt. I'd been used to taking hits all my life.

It wasn't the punches, elbows or knees that hurt or what did the damage. It was me. I hurt myself. I froze and shelled up.

The crowd was looking on, confused, perplexed as to what was happening. Fans, friends, coaches, and family couldn't make sense of what they saw.

This wasn't the fighter they knew.

But they couldn't hear my thoughts, the enemy within.

I was so afraid.

Afraid of being so tired.

Afraid of losing.

Afraid of not being me.

Afraid that I could never live up to the expectations placed upon me.

These became my dominant thoughts and, in turn, my actual reality.

The referee saw too many unanswered blows and quite rightly stopped the fight, declaring my opponent the victor.

I was instantly furious with myself. I jumped up and screamed in frustration at my embarrassing performance and how I had just quit on myself.

My own mind and will gave that victory away.

I let fear take over, and I chose to lose.

"A person who doubts himself is like a man who would enlist in the ranks of his enemies and bear arms against himself."

Alexander Dumas

My mind had turned on me.

But little would I know it was one of the most pivotal moments in all my career and an essential experience to help me understand not only my mind and thoughts but how to help so many others that I would coach.

As with so many things in our life that seem negative and detrimental to our triumphs, they often provide us with the blueprint to success later in life. Understanding how to reframe our fears and utilise them to help better our performance is a crucial tool many top performers and athletes use. We'll explore how, using a principle called Amor Fati, in chapter twelve.

RAMPAGE VS. JON JONES

I've had the honour and pleasure of coaching and competing against some of the finest athletes and performers in sport.

A great example and one I'm immensely proud of is all my time spent coaching former UFC and Pride FC light heavyweight champion Quinton "Rampage" Jackson.

In regular day-to-day life, Quinton is a lovely man. He is a caring, loyal friend and one of the funniest people you could meet. He is a larger than life character able to make light of many situations and who can own a room with his laugh and brilliant sense of humour.

Anyone who has enjoyed watching his interviews or has seen his tenure as a coach on the Ultimate Fighter series will attest to his joyous and childlike behaviours that endear him to many.

But this behaviour is a far cry from what those opponents across from the cage experience, where his "Rampage" persona is in full effect in the cage from the moment he walks into the cage with his big heavy chain around his neck, howling like a wolf as he slowly stalks his prey.

All who stood across his path feared him.

His knockouts from powerful punches were well-known to fans and fighters alike. His big slams, where he would pick people up above his head and slam them down onto the canvas and into unconsciousness, were all over the internet for anyone to watch.

No opponent could watch Rampage and think they'd have a nice night. He was terrifying, and everyone knew it.

One of those opponents facing Rampage was the undefeated champion Jon Jones. Rated by most as one of the greatest of all time in the sport, his exemplary performances and calmness under pressure, alongside his undefeated record, have cemented his status in the sport as a fighting great for all time.

The fight was a massive deal at the time. The UFC light heavyweight championship was on the line, and it was one of the most arduous fight camps I have ever been involved in.

We spent months developing and prepping Rampage for this bout.

Living in the fantastic, brand new Muscle Pharm facility in Denver, we had access to underwater treadmills, nutritionists tweaking meal plans and supplements, and oxygen chambers to assist in recovery whilst training at high altitude, which offers less available oxygen to your body, which, over time, creates a more efficient body able to perform under stress needing less oxygen. The training was extensive. We had prepared for this fight, and Rampage was in phenomenal shape.

After the arduous twelve-week training camp, the night of the bout arrived for these two amazing fighters.

The walkout was immense.

We walked to the cage as a team, walking through the sold-out crowd at the Pepsi Centre in Denver as Rampage's walkout music rang out around the arena. The whole crowd chanted.

"RAMPAGE, RAMPAGE, RAMPAGE!"

We arrived at the gates of the octagon, and Rampage stepped inside as his other coaches and I made our way around to the outside of the cage.

"God give me style, God give me grace . . . " the hit 50 Cent song fired up on the speakers, and the champion Jon Jones walked to the cage as the music changed into DDM's "Coming Home." The crowd went wild as Jon entered the cage.

The referee called the two men to the centre of the cage for their face-off. There are few as intense as Rampage in these stare-offs, and Jon Jones avoided eye contact and stared past him when they faced off. They headed back to their corners, and the referee actioned to begin the fight.

It was then that the strangest thing happened.

Jon crawled toward Rampage on all fours and stalked him down.

Rampage, myself, and the other coaches were perplexed at what he was doing. We had never seen a fight start like this in all our years.

Rampage tried to hit him, but Jon moved his head side to side, dodging the blows whilst perched on his hands and feet. Jon was crawling around like Spiderman, engaging his "Spidey sense" to avoid those punishing, heavy shots of Rampage's.

Then, around thirty seconds into the fight, Jon wrestled with Rampage, and the fight continued as usual.

It was a great battle that lasted until the fourth round, where Jon Jones retained his UFC title, winning with a rear naked choke.

For the longest time, I remained unsure why Jon had decided to engage Rampage in such a strange manner at the start of the bout.

I had never seen that happen in all my years involved in the sport.

Years later, I found out why.

Rampage's intense character and ferocity as a fighter had caused great concern for the champion. And rightly so. He was fearful of Rampage and of the amazing knockout power he possessed.

In his dreams, or more appropriately nightmares, he would see himself being knocked out by Rampage. He would see Rampage landing one of his signature knockout blows in the first thirty seconds of the bout.

The image was burned into his thoughts daily.

His visions showed the same outcome: a victorious Rampage over his unconscious body.

Years later, in an interview when talking about the bout, Jon said, "So, with Rampage Jackson, I kept having these nightmares that I would get knocked out, and no matter how the fight played out, I would always get knocked out.

"One scenario, he'd run at me, swing an overhand right.

The other, he'd throw a right uppercut. Another a left hook, and I couldn't avoid this inevitable knockout that I was going to experience—so I felt like I was going to get knocked out, and I felt like this was coming for me like a signal from a higher power.

"My idea to crawl toward him was the only thing that hadn't happened to me in all my nightmares. So something just said get on your knees and crawl up to him, and then, automatically, the dream voids itself immediately."

Powerful, empowering stuff.

Knowing that a world champion of the calibre and experience of Jon Jones would suffer with these kind of pre-fight nerves, the nightmares and restless nights, shows how prevalent pre-competition nerves are for us all.

No matter the competition.

No matter who you are.

As the saying goes, "We think our pain is unique, until we read."

We all suffer from the same pressures and thoughts, until we learn effective coping mechanisms and how employ them when they are needed.

Jones circumvented his nightmare vision and worked around it to his advantage in an extremely impressive way. He took back control and power by altering the dreams. His act of crawling towards Rampage not only helped him in his personal empowerment, but also confused Rampage and us, his corner team.

SUPERSTITION

"When you believe in things you don't understand, then you suffer. Superstition ain't the way."

Stevie Wonder

Stop and ask yourself if you're superstitious.

Think about what superstitions you hold on to that don't serve you.

Superstition has been around for a very long time.

It affects everyone who has them in their day-to-day lives.

It is believed that superstitions began in the early days of humanity, and we used and embraced them as a way to try to explain the unexplainable.

Natural disasters, thunderstorms, illness, and the like happening in an uncertain world, void of the information at our fingertips in the modern day. Superstition would have provided us a way of reasoning why or how things happened to us and our loved ones.

They may have assisted with fears of an unknown world, but looking closer, we can see how disempowering these superstitions are in our daily lives now.

How many people need the stereo volume at an even or odd number?

Those afflicted think along the lines of, *10 is too quiet, 12 is too loud, and 11 would be perfect, but it's an odd number, and if I put it on that, something terrible will happen, so I will decide to sit and listen more intently or turn it up too loud and damage my eardrum*s.

I know how it works because I lived it.

I see it happen with many others, too, in my coaching.

A loss attributed to not wearing the correct "lucky" underwear or because the scenario before fights or matches didn't play out exactly as envisioned.

Many fighters have attributed luck to a corner they are fighting out of: "When I was In the blue corner, I won last time. I performed exceptionally then, so I must be in the blue corner every fight, and then I will win."

To give that kind of power to an inanimate object and colour appears a little crazy, doesn't it, when reading it in black and white?

You're willing to say that your victory wasn't down to the years of hard work you and your coaches put in to develop your craft, but because of which colour corner you represented on that night?

Are you willing to pin your career's hopes, dreams, and future on the luck of being in the "correct" corner?

The issue with a reliance on superstition is if things don't go the way you expect they should because of the superstition, it throws us totally off the ability to be our best.

They take the onus off the athlete, performer, and business owner, allowing the superstitious belief to disempower them. The opportunity to grow, make mistakes, learn lessons, and embrace a growth mindset is removed; instead, blame is pinned on an external force.

It's great for our egos in the short term but not so great for us and our improvement and career as employing superstitions enables the victim mindset.

It removes us from being the creator, the victor, and it prevents us from being the ones who create action by putting us in a place of reacting to outside events.

In the long term, superstitions have always been more of a hindrance than providing a positive effect.

When looking at the origins of some of these superstitions and how they are created from fear and anguish, it's evident they often produce similar feelings within us.

Take the number 13, for instance.

The unlucky reputation of this number is connected to two distinct tales.

In the Last Supper, as depicted in the New Testament of the Bible, the thirteenth guest to arrive was Judas Iscariot, infamous for his betrayal. Judas identified Jesus to the religious authorities during the Passover meal, leading directly to Jesus' crucifixion.

Norse mythology offers a parallel story. The thirteenth guest, the mischievous god Loki, deceives and manipulates the blind god Hod, causing the death of the god Baldr with a mistletoe projectile.

Another superstition warns against opening an umbrella indoors. This belief finds its roots in ancient Egypt, where umbrellas, representing shade, were considered sacred. Using them indoors was seen as an affront to the sun god. In more modern times, the superstition also might relate to the practical concerns of breaking things inside.

The belief that walking under a ladder brings bad luck might have originated from the triangular shape it forms against a wall, symbolizing the Holy Trinity. More practically, avoiding walking under ladders might prevent things from falling on you or disrupting someone working atop it.

Regardless of the superstition's origins, we must be vigilant about the influence they exert on our behavior. Especially for leaders (and not just CEOs or coaches) but most notably parents. Children learn from our actions and our fears.

The adage, "Show me your five closest friends, and I'll predict your future," rings true, especially when the people children interact with most are their primary caregivers. If they observe parents fearing a lone magpie, believing it's an omen of doom, it's plausible they'll adopt similar beliefs.

Many superstitions are driven by fear, often a fear of the unknown. At a public speaking event, I was questioned about using superstition positively. The individual argued that having a lucky charm might boost confidence or performance levels. While this might seem advantageous, depending on such items can become problematic. If the lucky charm goes missing, does it now become unlucky? Is performance intrinsically linked to this object? If so, it's a detriment.

But establishing a personal ritual or mantra can be different. If you have a routine, words of affirmation, or a meditation practice to either calm or invigorate yourself, it's empowering because you're in control. As long as there's no outcome attached to the ritual.

For example, "I'll tap my hands ten times and then I'll succeed." Such practices to reach a peak state can be beneficial. As a coach, I prefer using routines, mantras, and breathwork to achieve peak or calmer states, whichever is desired, instead of relying on an external stimulus or, as is the case with superstitions, focusing on the outcome and not the processes.

CHAPTER 7
A FEAR OF SUCCESS

"To avoid criticism, say nothing, do nothing, be nothing."

Elbert Hubbard

It isn't just a fear of failure that prevents us from doing what we wish to do, but also the thought of succeeding.

At the surface level, it doesn't appear that we would fear being successful and achieving all we set out to do, but dig a little deeper, and it starts to make a little sense.

Many people learn, even as early as school, that people often don't like overachievers. We realise at a young age that sometimes to keep "friends," and I use that term loosely, we may have to play it down a little and play a little dumb.

When questions in class are asked, we don't want people to know we know the answer, so we keep our hands down to avoid bringing attention upon ourselves.

So often, it causes jealousy, envy, and hatred from our so-called friends because they can't cope with the spotlight not being on them.

They can't cope with the fact that you may achieve something, and they won't.

That you know something and they don't.

In the classic book *How to Win Friends and Influence People*, Dale Carnegie writes on the subject of friendship, quoting philosopher La Rochefoucauld: "If you want enemies, excel your friends; but if you want friends, let your friends excel you."

In friendship circles, this is known as the crabs in a bucket mentality. People love to commiserate, not so much to congratulate as egos don't get threatened or hurt when we are consoling people.

Have you ever seen crabs that when caught get placed in buckets and shipped off to the supermarket for us to buy and eat?

They pile them on top of each other, one after the other, to the top of the bucket. Literally rising high enough that the crabs could easily escape by gripping the edge of the bucket and pulling themselves out.

Many of them try so hard to get out, and there's one thing that stops them: their crab friends.

They see that their friend is going to escape the death sentence. They're going to go off to a better, free life, and they can't allow it, so they reach up with their claws and pull their 'friend' back into the bucket every time.

Every time.

The people around us can be no different.

They keep pulling us back into the bucket, and just because it isn't a physical bucket, it doesn't mean it's not happening.

As you wish to better your life and want more, sometimes those around you will wonder where this leaves them. They will question why you are able to achieve things while they aren't.

They may see your desire for more success as a nod that you care less for them. Possibly, they hold disdain and resentment toward your ambition.

But maybe it doesn't come from a jealous view, or at least to them, it doesn't appear that way. It can come from a confused perspective of love or what people mistakenly think love is.

If you achieve these goals, they think, where will they be? What will happen to your need for them? What if you change and you don't love them the same any longer?

This isn't real love, though.

It's fear masquerading as love.

Consider the man who purports to love a flower. If he sits with the flower, waters, and feeds it, and enjoying its beauty as it sits where it lays performing its predestined duty, he is sure to love it.

But if he wishes to keep all the beauty to himself and be the only one who loves the flower and, in doing so, uproots the flower and holds it tightly in his grasp, preventing anyone else ever seeing the beauty of the flower, until eventually there will be no beauty left. The flower will die, and the beauty will fade.

We might also fear what our success will bring us.

What implications might achieving success have on our future workload and expectations? What if the exceptional standard we've set now becomes the expected norm for all subsequent work?

If we believe we've given our absolute best, there's the daunting prospect of continuously maintaining that standard. The idea alone might seem overwhelming.

This apprehension can be seen as a subset of the fear of failure, albeit projected further into the future. We worry about what lies ahead: changing workloads, increased responsibilities, heightened competition, and the constant pressure to uphold a superior standard in our work.

PROCRASTINATION

Procrastination is a challenge many of us face when trying to accomplish our goals. It often manifests as a habitual delay, leading us to avoid essential tasks and actions, resulting in increased stress, missed opportunities, and unfulfilled potential.

Contrary to popular belief, procrastination isn't merely a result of poor time management or laziness. It's a deeper emotional response rooted in fear. Fears of success, failure, judgment, and the unknown can all drive us to procrastinate for various reasons.

Historically, if we've associated the outcome of a task with pain—be it ridicule, embarrassment, failure, or criticism from parents, teachers, or bosses—we might hesitate to embark on similar endeavors in the present. We don't want to commit fully to a task if we're unsure of the result or fear it might make us seem incompetent. Thus, we delay, hoping to stave off those potential negative outcomes.

We also fear threats to our self-worth. If we visualise past negative outcomes, we might employ procrastination as a defensive strategy.

After all, succeeding in one area can lead to more significant challenges: moving to a new location after a job offer, adjusting to new colleagues, meeting heightened expectations. Such successes could pave the way for increased responsibilities and, possibly, higher chances of failure as tasks become more demanding.

This cycle can make us question: is it better to remain stagnant and procrastinate, or to embrace the potential challenges that come with growth?

PERFECTION PARALYSIS

General George Patton once said, "A good plan today is better than a perfect one tomorrow."

The more you aim solely for perfection, the longer it will take you to achieve your targets, and the more you will procrastinate.

The need for perfection can stop you from writing your book, delivering that speech, entering that competition, or just taking a leap of faith as you chase your dreams.

You'd be shocked how many times I've spoken to people desperate to start their martial arts or fitness training, only to have them say, "I'll get fit first, before I start."

When the topic of joining a gym for classes or weightlifting emerges, they frequently stall. They're held back by a mental image of where they believe they need to be before beginning–

an image so daunting that they never make that initial move. All they'd need is one foot in the door and the realisation that whatever their current fitness state, it can be enhanced.

Using "perfection" as a shield protects our ego and fuels our procrastination tendencies. The concept of perfection, being inherently elusive, offers a convenient shield against external judgment. This incessant need to be flawless intertwines with our apprehensions about failure, which only bolsters our tendency to procrastinate. Though it offers a surface-level comfort of alibis, deep within, it fosters self-discontent, self-doubt, and self-criticism. This further chips away at our self-assuredness, intensifying the paralysing fear of failure, and consequently steering us into an unending spiral of procrastination.

Realising that "done is better than perfect" is crucial in freeing you from procrastination.

A book written can constantly be improved.

A talk continually added to and taken away from.

A piece of art held on to for little additions for all time.

If something is off slightly when you receive feedback, utilise it in the next project . Naturally, your quality of work increases through the lessons you learn and your competence increases along the way.

Remember, *Competence breeds confidence.*

IMPOSTER SYNDROME

The imposter syndrome is a great collection of all these fears we've been exploring. It prays on our fear of failure and success at the same time, making it particularly vicious.

Those suffering from Imposter syndrome, despite their outstanding accomplishments and massive achievements, allow themselves to feel like a fraud or at least have the fear of being outed as one.

Studies have shown that around seventy percent of the population has or does suffer from imposter syndrome at some time in their lives.

Many of us have suffered from it, especially at times of stress or when feeling overwhelmed, like in a new job role, or at times of vulnerability, like giving a talk or teaching a class on a subject to other people.

We may even try to convince ourselves of being frauds, damage ourselves and our chances of success with self-sabotaging behaviours like self-doubt, limiting beliefs and even physical actions like drinking too much alcohol or drug abuse.

It can affect anyone, regardless of their actual accomplishments, skills, and competency.

How many times have you heard tales of the "could have been?"

I could've played for Manchester, but . . .

I could've been an Olympic athlete, but . . .

I was going to be *this*, until *that* happened . . .

We have all heard tales like this, and it's certainly possible that they could have been these things, but there is always a reason why they weren't. An injury, a life-changing event, something in the way—but it is always something external as opposed to being their own doing that somehow stops them.

I have met many talented martial artists in my time as a fighter and even more so as a coach.

Their whole identity is associated with being good at this sport/career or study, and they've had the displeasure of having "yes men" surround them from an early age. Pressure is unknowingly applied by parents who talk of the dizzying heights their offspring will reach because they are so good at something. Creating a burdening weight on their shoulders that they must aim to live up to and an image to uphold.

These kids come to fear their failure or success so much that the only way off this train is an injury or some event that derails them and makes it okay to stop. Okay that they failed, and okay that they can't do it anymore.

You see it with the bigger kids—those who are so much bigger and more athletic than the others when they are young. Playing rugby or a physical sport, they are able to power through those less developed, younger children.

It seems easy to them, and their whole identity is pinned on being bigger and better than the other children. But it doesn't last. The other kids eventually and obviously grow too, and now it isn't so easy to them anymore.

As they enter their late teens and early adulthood, they realise there are other players or athletes who bit down and pushed through those difficult days when they were smaller and developed through adversity daily by working on their skills. The smaller, less athletic kids were afforded the luxury of building and developing their resilience and of facing up to failing and learning.

As they begin to face challenges, the once effortless task of excelling in their sport now feels like a struggle. Their identity has become intertwined with their athletic abilities, leading to a dislike for the pressure of meeting expectations. Imposter syndrome sets in, and the cracks begin to show. Unknowingly, they have adopted a fixed mindset and let their fears hinder their growth and development throughout their adult life.

For every difficulty, fear and anxiety inducing incident I have faced, I have created a blueprint filled with effective solutions to combat the ill effects of being fearful, which transformed my life in to one that is Fearless by Design.

In the following chapters, I will reveal them to you so you are able to do the same.

CHAPTER 8
COPING MECHANISMS

"He who makes no mistakes, makes no progress."

Teddy Roosevelt

I think it's pretty safe to say that we have all struggled with our minds, self-talk, self-perception, limiting beliefs, anxiety, depression, and other mental health issues and concerns.

You are not alone. Whatever you or a loved one are currently going through, know that among the nearly eight billion people in the world right now and the plethora of people throughout history, there will have been another person who has gone through similar circumstances or problems.

Superstars, athletes, medalists, entrepreneurs, managers, accountants—whatever the role, many of the most successful and highest achieving people in the world utilise one or many of the

following coping mechanisms I'm about to show
you to help achieve their success.

What is a coping mechanism?

Coping mechanisms are essentially a plan of
action or a set of guidelines that people follow in
times of emotional turmoil, particularly during
high levels of stress and anxiety. In psychological
terms, coping mechanisms usually fall into one of
two categories: Problem-focused and emotion-
focused.

Problem-focused coping is all about dealing
with the source of your stress head-on. For
example, if you're facing a challenging exam that
you're not confident about, you'd use problem-
focused coping to seek out tutoring and perhaps
extend your study hours each week. This
approach aims to tackle the issue directly, offering
tangible solutions.

On the flip side, emotion-focused coping
focuses on managing your emotional responses.
This strategy is especially useful in situations that
are beyond your control, such as the loss of a
loved one. Here, you could turn to practices like
meditation, as taught by the Stoics, to help
manage your emotional state.

As we dive deeper into these coping
mechanisms, it's vital to comprehend that to reap
the most benefits in our daily lives, we must fully

commit to practicing them. Think of it like physical fitness. If you aim to build a strong, muscular, and healthy body, consistent and regular gym visits are non-negotiable. Over time, as your body adapts to the training regimen, you'll need to ramp up the intensity to continue making progress.

In the same vein, these coping mechanisms can transform your life but only if you integrate them into a structured routine. Meditation, for instance, can empower you to control your thoughts, but one session won't cut it. The key lies in consistent practice that fits seamlessly into your daily routine.

The benefits of these practices are not limited to immediate relief; they extend into all aspects of your life. Daily disciplined practice brings long-term rewards, granting you a sense of calm and tranquility. So, choose your preferred coping mechanisms and strive to practice them daily for optimal results.

Lastly, understanding when to engage these "states," whether fight or flight or rest and digest, is crucial. It's entirely natural to experience heightened alertness in situations like competitive events, where an adrenaline rush can be beneficial. Conversely, it's counterproductive to be in a heightened state when trying to sleep or relax. Learning to discern between different emotional needs and how to activate them at will can be a tremendous asset.

CHAPTER 9
STOICISM

*"First say to yourself what you would be:
and then do what you have to do."*

Epictetus

Who would have thought that today, in the
twenty-first century, Stoicism—a philosophy
thousands of years old—would offer solutions for
our modern struggles with poor mental health,
depression, and anxiety?

It's crucial to distinguish between "stoic," a
term often used to describe someone as
emotionless or suppressing feelings, and
Stoicism, the philosophical school of thought. In
Stoicism, the goal isn't to eliminate emotion but to
avoid negative and unconstructive feelings, such
as jealousy or anger.

This ancient philosophy emphasises virtues
like self-mastery, discipline, and a focus on what's
within one's control. These tenets have found a
place in modern treatments, notably Cognitive

Behavioral Therapy (CBT), and are especially beneficial for individuals dealing with anxiety and depression.

The inception of Stoicism dates back to the life experiences of its founder, Zeno of Citium. A former wealthy merchant, Zeno found himself in Athens in 300 BCE after a shipwreck left him financially ruined. Looking for meaning and direction, he was drawn to the philosophical teachings of Socrates, which stress the importance of self-examination, ethical living, and wisdom.

Under the tutelage of Crates of Thebes, a leading Cynic philosopher, Zeno adopted some aspects of Cynicism. However, he also wanted to craft a philosophy that was more reasoned and systematic. A visit to the Oracle of Delphi and an enigmatic directive led him to "take on the colour of the dead," which he interpreted as studying the works of great but deceased philosophers. After absorbing the works of pre-Socratic philosopher Heraclitus and others, Zeno went on to develop Stoicism.

The Stoics, named after the Stoa Poikile where they gathered, have left a lasting impact on philosophy and mental health practices. While the origins may be ancient, the relevance of Stoicism in today's world is anything but obsolete. It serves as a practical tool for self-improvement and emotional resilience, continuing to inspire and aid people from all walks of life.

Looking at who has embraced and utilised Stoicism throughout history, we can see an extensive array of diverse people employing this philosophy as a way of life.

Marcus Aurelius, the last of the great Roman emperors, was an avid Stoic, as can be seen in his journal Meditations—a book compiling all of his thoughts (and a book that he never intended for public reading). Nevertheless, the book is filled with amazing quotes, thoughts, feelings, opinions, and scenarios, all with Stoic undertones.

We will look at how we can embrace part of Stoic teachings and ideals, alongside aiming to live a virtuous life with a few of the concepts I embrace personally from the Stoics. Let's start with a collection of various quotes and thoughts from some of the great Stoic minds we have had the pleasure of learning from.

Epictetus, a former slave mistreated by his masters who later became a free man, is one of the finest examples of a person utilising Stoicism to develop strong character and will.

From his teachings, it was apparent he cared little about others' opinions about him and thought everyone else should do the same. He believed that focusing on our own actions and not the actions of others assists us in being free.

His written teachings, *The Enchiridion*, famously mention what is under our control.

"Some things are in our control and others not. Things in our control are opinion, pursuit, desire, aversion, and, in a word, whatever are our own actions. Things not in our control are body, property, reputation, command, and, in one word, whatever are not our own actions."

This leads us to our first rule perfectly.

STOIC RULE NUMBER ONE: POWER OVER YOUR RESPONSE, NOT OUTSIDE EVENTS

How often are we triggered or upset by an event or person? Things totally out of our control, and yet we still allow these events to control us and affect us.

Driving somewhere, we hit traffic, causing us to be at a standstill. We rage and fume over the possibility of being late or missing an appointment.

We imagine these disastrous outcomes—missing appointment times, possibly being late, or getting annoyed at being stuck on a road when we desperately want to be home. Instead of remaining calm and accepting that there is nothing we can do to alter the outcome, we get even more frustrated and angry.

Instead, we should be aiming to understand that, as far as the traffic goes, it is totally out of our control. There is nothing we can do to alter the flow of traffic when we are stuck in the middle of it.

Other things *are* in our control. If our concern is being late, we can call ahead and let those we are meeting know how sorry we are. There has obviously been an accident of some sort, and it has caused us to be late on our journey, and we will get there as soon as our journey permits and devise a plan that suits our new, estimated arrival time. Furthermore, we could take advantage of our extra time to possibly plan or relax as we wait.

Illness, the economy, or even bad weather are all often out of our control. So why be upset, annoyed, frustrated, or succumb to any other negative emotion around something that you are unable to alter?

The world-famous serenity prayer utilised around the world by members of Alcoholics Anonymous delivers this same concept.

"God, grant me the serenity to accept the things I cannot change, the courage to change the things I can, and the wisdom to know the difference."

The influence of Stoicism on Reinhold Niebuhr when he penned the prayer was evident.

When I first began public speaking, I often allowed my imagination to be overactive. Sometimes, I would be overly concerned about how my information would be received and how the viewers and listeners would take to the talk and content.

Then I remembered I must practice what I preach and teach.

I knew the content I would deliver and how it would help many people. I already had great feedback and many messages of thanks and gratitude for the help my content had given those in need, but I was still too concerned about how the content would be received.

I knew that I had done my best. I had researched the content thoroughly. I had lived my life learning and employing this content and, in turn, coaching some of the most successful people in their chosen fields with these same concepts.

I couldn't control how people would take these talks and how they would, if ever, use the information I was teaching them.

It is precisely the same with a book. We can only control the content, not how many people buy the book or how many rave about it, criticise it, or rate it negatively.

Once the book is finished and out there, nothing else can be done to it. But what else could be done if the best effort was put in throughout the writing process, instead of spent worrying about the aftermath?

Viktor Frankl was a Jewish psychologist who became a prisoner in the Nazi death camps and wrote the hugely successful book *Man's Search for Meaning.*

In it the book, Frankl describes how man needs meaning, and it is this that provides our motivation to act as described by his logotherapy.

"We have absolutely no control over what happens to us in life, but what we have paramount control over is how we respond to those events."

Viktor Frankl

We also read similar sentiments from Stephen Covey, the author of *The Seven Habits of Highly Effective People*.

"Between stimulus and response, there is a space. In that space is our power to choose our response. In our response lies our growth and our freedom."

Stephen R Covey

When you adopt this mindset of caring about what is under your control, or when you begin to use the serenity prayer with faith and understanding, your anxiety rate will diminish, and your productivity will accelerate. You are setting an intention of concentrating on your desired actions and outcomes, leading you to your desired goal.

STOIC RULE NUMBER TWO: IS THIS THE CONDITION I SO FEARED?

The life of a martial artist or fighter can be very lonely with very little financial support and stability.

In my quest to become the greatest martial artist I possibly could, financial gain and prosperity took a back seat in my life. When my focus was on developing my skills and fitness, it left me very little time to establish a "career" or anything that would lead me to amass a fortune.

Travelling to train with the best I could find daily would lead to fees in train and bus travel and training expenses, which would consume most of our money. I would work as a personal trainer and a martial arts teacher and coach, but while training to compete, these roles needed to take a back seat.

Fortunately, my wife also worked, and we got by in our lovely home.

When I look back to the times when my wife needed to carry a calculator with her when she went grocery shopping to be sure not to overspend, I do so with fondness because we were still very happy in a loving home. Admittedly, it may have been a little cold due to no central heating, but we loved it all the same.

These times taught me how happy we can be with very little.

I won't lie or pretend; I enjoy the abundance my life blesses me with now, and every day, I am grateful for it all, but I also know I can be happy in times of hardship, too. Struggling financially taught me many incredible lessons that have helped me numerous times in developing my philosophy. However, it taught me I can go without a lot and still be happy.

But hindsight is twenty-twenty, and I would be stretching the truth if I were to say that at the time, all those years ago, I didn't have some sleepless nights and bouts of stress concerned about our financial situation. I would fear the awful outcomes that could happen if we had no money and couldn't pay for what we needed.

But one day, I came across the stoic teachings, most notably those of the philosopher Seneca. In particular, this quote spoke to me deeply.

"Set aside a certain number of days, during which you shall be content with the scantiest and cheapest fare, with course and rough dress, saying to yourself the while: 'Is this the condition that I feared?'"

As my thoughts on having no money would linger, causing more fear and panic, I imagined how it would feel not to be able to eat. To not have money to buy food . To go hungry.

But Seneca's words started to shift how I would approach all things I feared:

"It is precisely in times of immunity from care that the soul should toughen itself beforehand for occasions of greater stress and it is while fortune is kind that I should fortify itself against her violence."

So, how can we utilise this concept to assist us in coping with our fears and anxieties?

We start with questions.

Question: What is the cause of my anxiety?

Answer: *A lack of money*

Question: What would be the worst thing if money was low?

Answer: *I wouldn't have money to buy food to eat.*

Question: How would that feel if you couldn't eat for a day or more?

Answer: I'm not sure. Let's find out.

So, I began fasting. No food, just water for a few days.

Nowadays, the practice has become adopted by many for its physiological benefits and positive influence on health markers through a process known as autophagy. In simplified terms, autophagy is where your body, upon being restricted from new energy sources, looks to older, damaged cells within your body and strips them down to utilise and form new ones.

At the time, I was unaware of time-restricted eating's many benefits. I just did it to face a fear and challenge and see how well I could cope.

I decided to fast for five full days whilst continuing my training. I found the fast straightforward and faced the expected ups and downs during the five days. I had times of heightened energy, along with bursts of mental acuity. Other times, I felt like I had no energy left for the day.

The thing I feared most became a powerful tool. Unbeknown to me then, I would embrace the art of fasting and time-restricted eating in my life regularly.

My fears, it turned out, were unfounded, and I was glad to face them and realise that my imagination, like many times before, had made things appear way worse than they were in reality.

Continuing to read Seneca's letter to his friend Lucillius, I was taken by how he also warned his friend not to feel great pride in what he was doing, reminding him that many suffer unwillingly daily.

"There is no reason however, why you should think that you are doing anything great: for you will be merely doing what many thousands of poor slaves and many thousands of poor men are doing every day. But you may credit yourself with this item, that you will not be doing it under compulsion, and that it will be as easy for you to endure it permanently as to make the experiment from time to time. Let us become intimate with poverty, so that fortune may not catch us off our guard.

We shall be rich with all the more comfort, if we once learn how far poverty is from being a burden."

The fear of many things happens to us because of the unknown, the unexpected. Facing these fears by tackling them head-on, and removing the unknown through purposeful exposure, empowers us and sets us free.

It also helps us embody the gratitude mindset, which we'll cover in a later chapter. We shall be rich with all the more comfort when we realise that we are blessed with all that we have.

STOIC RULE NUMBER THREE: MEMENTO MORI

"You could leave life right now. Let that determine what you do and say and think."

Marcus Aurelius

Remember that you must die.

That is what the Latin phrase, *Memento Mori*, means.

It may sound morbid or a little depressing at first glance (especially to Westerners). In our modern Western society, death and even talk about it tends to be hidden away until there is no way of hiding it anymore. On those sad days that catch us all, which involve the death of a loved one or a horrific worldwide event that shows us the fragility of life.

We all remember that tragic, awful day of 9/11 and where we were when we heard or saw the terrible scenes as we thought and prayed for all of those two thousand nine hundred ninety-seven victims and their poor families.

When death is revealed to us in this manner, we seemingly, fleetingly, become aware of our own mortality. We realise how limited our time is and, in turn, how precious it all is. We are quick to let our loved ones know how much they mean to us. We ponder our past failings and successes and strive and promise to achieve more than we have so far. We will be better, do better, and work harder at everything we do.

Then, for most, life and its daily routine gradually seem to get in the way again, and those thoughts get pushed back to another day.

Many Eastern cultures, religions, and spiritualists have a much different view on death than we do in the West. Its acceptance is talked about much more and seen in their lives.

The Stoics, however, knew and accepted that death was inevitable and could come at any time as well.

The Latin phrase was initially used in ancient Rome and would be uttered by the slaves of the Roman generals as they would enjoy their victory parades.

"Remember, you're just a man," They would whisper, as they observed their masters bathing in their glory, intended to prevent their leaders' hubris and subsequent downfall from their prideful boasts and exhalations from the supporting crowds.

This a stark reminder that, despite their successes, they are indeed just a man and should not become consumed by excessive pride and self-worth.

Many in modern society may see Memento Mori as depressing. But if you alter the perspective, you will see how freeing it is.

Are you worried about failing?

Are you concerned about others judging you?

Are you embarrassed about something?

Guilty over something?

As harsh as this sounds, so what?

Eventually, no one will care; that's if they even do right now.

Because one day you will die.

And so will they.

The Romans would also carry a coin with "Memento Mori" inscribed into it as a daily reminder of life's fragility and how it will all be over and forgotten someday.

Why do we allow thoughts of others' opinions to prevent us from taking chances when, like Marcus Aurelius points out, we all end up in the same place? We know how selfish it is of us to hold ourselves back. Our hopes, our dreams, and our visions could change and empower the whole world if we got out of our own way.

Imagine the power of the business that needs starting, the book that needs writing, that job that needs applying for. We must move and be complicit in the motives of the universe, assist in the plans that God has in store for us, and strive to give our best.

The graveyard is a treasure trove.

It is filled with riches beyond our comprehension.

The greatest stories never told.

The wisdom never passed on.

The songs never sung.
The deep love never given.
The book never written.
The teacher that never taught.
The business never built.
The medicine never made.
The risk never taken.
Gone forever, never seen, because of fear.
Because of what ifs.

If you have a gift, a dream, or a vision, you not only owe it to yourself, but to the whole world, to set out and do it.

If not now, then when?
If not you, then who?

STOIC RULE NUMBER FOUR: AMOR FATI

What if everything you've endured—the obstacles, the trials, the hardships—wasn't accidental but purposeful, molding you into the individual the universe intended? The person the world desperately needs. Could you look at each challenge not as a burden but as a necessary part of your journey, even a gift?

This is the essence of the Latin term "Amor Fati": the love of one's fate.

The Stoics grasped the perpetual flux of the universe, acknowledging the vital role of change. They emphasised the importance of embracing life's ever-shifting conditions instead of resisting them. Your perception of these events, more than the events themselves, profoundly affects your experience.

Life's struggles and obstacles can be profound learning opportunities. What may seem unbearable at the moment often serves as a catalyst propelling you to where you're most needed. Consider the job you despised but lost a year ago. It felt devastating at the time, leaving you without income or visible prospects. Yet now, you find yourself in a dream role you wouldn't have dared to pursue otherwise.

Or think about the relationship that ended, shattering your heart and your belief in love. Now, you're united with the partner of your dreams. Every ending, be it a job, a relationship, or even a friendship, leads to a new beginning.

The love for what life throws at us is not just about embracing the good but also valuing the challenges, for each brings its own set of lessons if we choose to seek them. By facing each obstacle head-on, we evolve into more resilient versions of ourselves.

Though Marcus Aurelius didn't use the term "Amor Fati" explicitly—he wrote in Greek, not Latin—his philosophies resonate strongly with the concept. By loving our fate, we are better positioned to navigate life's complexities, forever evolving and adapting. And in doing so, we become the person we were always meant to be, the person the universe—and the world—needs.

> *"All that is in accord with you is in accord with me, O world! Nothing which occurs at the right time for you comes too soon or too late for me. All that your seasons produce, o nature, is fruit for me."*

In more modern times, German philosopher Fredrich Nietzsche embraced the concept of Amor Fati: "My formula for greatness in a human being is amor fati, that one wants nothing to be different, not forward, not backward, not in all eternity, not merely bear what is necessary, but love it."

At the exact moment, we can never tell why something is happening to us or for us. We can only foresee its true purpose long after the event.

Consider Peter (not his real name), a professional fighter. His sole aim? To become a

UFC world champion. He abandoned a regular job, choosing instead to hone his fighting skills under the tutelage of his devoted coach. They were more than just fighter and coach; they were like father and son, bound by the shared dream of reaching the pinnacle of the fighting world.

With each fight, Peter gained not just victories but invaluable experience, climbing from amateur ranks to professional fights. Multiple championships followed, and it seemed the UFC was just a call away. But then the unexpected happened.

A routine brain scan revealed an abnormality— an AVM (Arteriovenous Malformation).

A tangle of blood vessels that connect arteries and veins in the brain. Many people could go their whole lives without ever knowing they have one, but for Peter, needing in-depth scans for his fighting career meant that this showed up.

After being informed of this AVM, Peter was told he wouldn't be cleared to fight. An AVM can be dangerous to regular people sometimes, but to a combat athlete, I think it's pretty apparent the dangers it poses. Taking head trauma with an AVM is a perilous proposition, so there was no way any doctor would give clearance for Peter to fight.

Peter was pulled out from his most significant fight ever, and his career hung in the balance.

"What do I do?"

"Where do I get treatment?"

"Will I ever get to compete again?"

Peter and his coach were inundated with questions, doubts, and fears. After hitting several brick walls, a glimmer of hope appeared in the form of radiosurgery—a non-invasive procedure to deal with the AVM. The catch? It would take three long years to know if the procedure was successful.

Could you fathom the mental fortitude required to wait for three years? Peter continued to train rigorously, keeping faith in his dream even as he saw others chase theirs.

Then came the disheartening news—the radiosurgery had failed to fully eradicate the AVM. The only remaining option was brain surgery, an invasive procedure with its own set of risks but a higher success rate than that of radiotherapy.

Brain surgery it was. After enduring weeks of darkness, intense headaches, and emotional turmoil, Peter was finally free of his AVM. Yet another hurdle presented itself—convincing a medical community skeptical of combat sports that he was fit to fight.

After months of uphill battles, Peter was cleared. He returned to the ring in a local show, putting on an electrifying performance and claiming victory.

The adversity he faced, the hurdles he overcame, his resilience—he was the living embodiment of Amor Fati. Peter's incredible journey serves as an inspiring testament to the transformative power of embracing one's fate.

The story is still being written. And one day, when Peter wraps that championship belt around his waist, the world will finally grasp the full scope of his incredible journey, a journey that was, in many ways, destined.

If not now, then when?

If not you, then who?

MAYBE

There is an old Zen tale of a farmer with an amazing horse. It's the most fantastic horse and is the talk of all who see it, and one night, it bolts free of its stable and runs off into the forest.

"*Oh, no*," says the farmer's neighbour. "It's so sad that your prized horse has run away."

"Maybe," calmly replies the farmer.

Early the following day, while carrying out his farm duties, the farmer hears a voice shouting to him in the distance.

"Father! Come quick." His son shouts to him, and the farmer runs to him to check what the noise is about.

As he reaches his son, he points to his prized horse returning to the farm and bringing four more horses from the wild along with it.

"Amazing father. Isn't it so lucky we not only get our horse but we also get new horses, too?"

"Maybe," the farmer replies.

The next day, the farmer is alerted by his neighbour.

"Come quickly, it's your son."
The farmer rushes to his son's aid as he sees him in pain, laying on the ground with a broken leg. "I fell from the horse, Father."

As the young boy was trying to train one of their newly acquired horses, the horse got a little afraid and threw the boy off his back, causing him to fall and break his leg.

The local doctor is called to attend to the boy, and upon leaving, he says to the farmer: "It is so unlucky that your son was thrown from that horse and has now broken his leg, isn't it?"

"Maybe." Came the reply.

Weeks go by. Then one day, the army comes to the farm, conscripting for the war. They needed young, healthy men to go to battle for their country.

When the recruiting officers see the farmer's son is bedridden with an injury, they leave the farm, knowing he will be unable to serve in the war.

"Unbelievable," says the neighbour on hearing the news. "You and your son are so lucky for him not to need to go to war."

"Maybe."

STOIC RULE NUMBER FIVE: PREMEDITATIO MALORUM

NEGATIVE VISUALISATION

We have already seen the efficacy and power of visualisation when it is utilised in learning and adapting to new skills. In chapter four, we saw how it improved basketball free throws specifically.

However, this particular visualisation technique is unique and distinct. The premeditation of evils is a powerful practice that

The Stoics referred to as "premeditatio malorum," or negative visualisation, which involves mentally preparing for potential challenges and setbacks. It which entails envisioning and contemplating an undesired scenario.

The death of a loved one. (The Romans seemingly dealt with death a lot.)

Illness. (The Antonine plague ravaged Rome during the great emperor Marcus Aurelius' reign.)

Loss of business. (Like Zeno and his shipwrecked cargo).

Loss of power or any other ills that may befall them.

The Stoics would sit and think about what they feared and didn't want to happen. Then from those thoughts, they would be led into scenarios where they would plan precisely how to deal with the situation. Through visualising these difficulties in advance, they developed a more resilient and balanced mindset that would be better equipped to handle adversity when it occurs.

Imagine a person who is about to embark on a new project at work. Applying the principle of premeditatio malorum, they would take some time to sit quietly and visualise potential obstacles or setbacks that could arise during the course of the project, like unforeseen delays or disagreements with colleagues. But by imagining these challenges vividly, they would be mentally preparing themselves to face adversity with composure and rationality.

Doing this can assist us in creating distance between the initial emotional reaction and our response, which might be something we prefer to avoid. This mental rehearsal can assist in us cultivating a sense of inner tranquility and equanimity even in the face of difficulty.

Also, this Stoic practice enables us to foresee any potential issues and devise contingency plans and strategies to overcome obstacles through envisioning what could go wrong. This can help reduce the associated anxiety linked to uncertainty and can help bolster confidence in facing and handling adverse situations.

As the name suggests, negative visualisation may appear negative, but it offers many positive possibilities. It can also leads us to one of the most powerful tools we have at our disposal within our toolbox of skills: gratitude.

CHAPTER 10
GRATITUDE

"Gratitude is the attitude."

Sterling K Brown

When we dread what we'd rather not happen, it becomes even easier to use one of the most powerful tools for changing our state of mind: gratitude.

Also, it opens the way to receive more into our lives.

When we have sat and feared the death of a loved one, and we then adopt an attitude of gratitude, we allow ourselves to show them fully our love and feelings as we realise they won't be around forever. And it's essential that not only do they know how much we love them, but we *feel* it deeply too. We feel truly grateful for their love and them being in our lives.

We can't simultaneously sit in a pit of fear while embracing gratitude. The two are mutually exclusive. They can't coexist. And that's a good thing, a liberating thing.

When we shift our focus, feel blessed for all that we have and are capable of, all the experiences we've had and the people who've touched our lives, it's like switching on a light in a dark room. We become aware of the endless possibilities around us. The hope. The magic of life that's always been there but was previously concealed by our fears and anxieties.

The possibilities.

The hope.

"Gratitude turns what we have into enough."

Melody Beattie

For those who journal regularly—and I can't recommend journaling enough—many will probably incorporate some form of gratitude into their daily entries. And that's fantastic, a step in the right direction. But it's also crucial to take that gratitude out of the pages and express it openly— to the universe, to God, to the people who make your life worth living.

As a family, we have this wonderful ritual. We sit at the dining table for our meals, and before diving into the food, we each share three things we're grateful for that day. This simple yet profound act not only allows us to acknowledge our blessings but also prompts us to dig deep into why these things matter to us. It's not just a cursory, surface-level thankfulness but an invitation to explore the roots of our gratitude.

While we're on the subject, it's essential to talk about the perils of superficial gratitude. Yes, it's easy to say you're grateful for this and that, list items off like you're ticking boxes—family, friends, food, finances, opportunities, and so on. However, if that gratitude isn't coming from a place of true feeling, it's empty, it's hollow. And this is where we fall short.

Feeling is the secret.

Sometimes, we go about our day, muttering thanks for seemingly trivial things. Like being thankful for our smartphones. And that's okay, but adding context and depth makes it more meaningful.

For example, today, *I am grateful for my smartphone because* it keeps me connected to the people I care about. It enables me to engage in personal growth, listen to audiobooks, communicate *with* loved ones, and even work remotely. This isn't just a piece of technology; it's a conduit for experiences, for growth, for connection.

Taking time to analyse why we're thankful can take a simple object or concept and elevate it to something that genuinely resonates with our souls.

To illustrate the importance of gratitude, consider this analogy. When someone takes the time to make you a cup of tea, your reaction determines whether you'll be offered that hospitality again in the future. A genuine display of gratitude not only fosters goodwill but also invites more of the same kindness in the future. This is how the universe works, my friends.

Gratitude is one of the most potent mood lifters and state changers you can tap into. When that internal voice tries to bring you down, focuses on the negative, or wallows in self-pity, it can be incredibly empowering to list what you're genuinely thankful for.

So even when it seems like you've hit rock bottom, remember there's always something to be grateful for. Always.

The old saying, "I cried because I had no shoes until I saw a man with no feet," makes a valid point. It urges us to look around and count our blessings, regardless of our current circumstances.

"Acknowledging the good that you already have in your life is the foundation for all abundance."

Eckhart Tolle

CHAPTER 11
REFRAMING

"Our key to transforming anything lies in our ability to reframe it."

Marianne Williamson

Reframing can be defined as transforming a negative belief into a positive one by choosing alternative words. Simply put, it involves using different vocabulary to alter one's perspective.

Take this for our first example:

EXCITEMENT

You and a friend decide to take a day out to the local theme park and go on the largest roller coaster there.

You're both in the queue waiting for your turn, and you can hear all the screams of the other park visitors as they whizz past.

Your friend is a massive fairground ride fan. But you? Not so much.

The further down the queue you get, the more the adrenaline is pumping, and you find yourself in fight or flight mode. Your stomach empties of surrounding blood, your pupils dilate, your heartbeat is pounding, and you start to sweat.

You look at your friend, who has a smile from ear to ear. They're the epitome of serenity, while you feel like it's the end of the world.

Yet, you're both going through the same physiological changes and reactions. You're both in the same place, in the same queue in the same theme park. Their heart rate has increased. They're breathing harder, shallower, and taking in all the experience, but they aren't fearful like you.

They're excited.

Your bodies are performing the same response. You are just interpreting the signals very differently.

If we are in a dangerous situation, we *want* to be in fight or flight mode. It is integral for our safety that we are at our peak performance in these high-risk situations.

But not when we are safe and not in need of its physiological benefits.

Do you remember Christmas Eve when you were a child?

If you're a parent, you won't need to remember; you will see it each Christmas with your children, too.

No matter the family tradition, it became difficult to drift off when it came time to sleep as we waited for Santa. We would think about Father Christmas descending the chimney and leaving plenty of gifts by the fireplace.

Our minds raced with imagined Christmas mornings, opening numerous gifts alongside our loved ones. And it would be early morning before any of us could get to sleep

It wasn't fear that kept us awake.

We weren't afraid of Santa Clause or even a stranger in our house.

We were excited.

Excited that he was finally coming.

Excited for all the things he would be bringing us.

Picture the day before a big job interview.

The nerves and excitement keep you awake— the worrying and stressing over the outcome instead of allowing yourself to be excited about the challenge.

We focus on our need to get the job instead of being able to concentrate on performing to our best in the interview.

Often, we focus on the feeling of being afraid of a perceived, undesired outcome instead of allowing the excitement of possibilities to lift us.

LETTER CHANGE

When we alter how we view tasks and opportunities by adopting a new perspective, we can assist ourselves in changing our physiological state.

Even changing something as simple as a letter in a word can alter the emotion and feeling in a sentence.

"I've *got* to go to the gym."

This insinuates being forced to do something out of your control. Something you would rather not do, but it *must* be done.

Compare that sentence with this sentence, when all we do is change the O to an E.

"I GET to go to the gym."

With one letter change, instantly the emotion in the sentence is altered as we speak it, incorporating the gratitude we mentioned earlier while empowering us because we "choose" to go to the gym.

I used this reframing technique a lot after being so severely injured and bedridden that I wasn't capable of being physical. I was desperate to get a sweat on, lift weights, or do a jiu-jitsu class. I promised myself then that if I were blessed enough to heal and allowed to return to the gym, I would embrace every opportunity.

When we use this type of reframe alongside other mechanisms, we can also see how much they can accentuate and complement each other. Imagine having some quiet time. You're reading a great book, when you realise you must put the book down to pick up your child from school.

You get up sluggish and reluctantly grab your keys.

You leave the house and begrudgingly go to get your child. Knowing you'll have to deal with other parents who are likely to ignore you, maybe gossip about you, (remember though, we don't care about their opinions), and possibly look rather miserable as they all wait at the gates for their children.

Or we can utilise this reframing alongside the Stoic method of Premeditatio Malorum to quickly change our state of negativity.

What about when your child is too old for school?

What if they no longer want you to pick them up because they want to show their independence?

What if, even worse, your child didn't go to school anymore?

What about when the time comes, and you can NEVER pick them up again?

Suddenly, "I get to" becomes an even easier philosophy to embrace.

I get to see my son's face as I ask him how his day was and what great new things that he learned that day.

I get to show him exactly how much he means to me and his importance to me and my life.

He knows my gratitude as I get to collect him from school.

CRITICISM

"To avoid criticism, say nothing, do nothing, be nothing."

Elbert Hubbard

Criticism.

As soon as you hear the word, it seems to get your back up, doesn't it?

The full definition of the word sounds awful: "The expression of disapproval of someone or something based on perceived faults or mistakes."

How often are we hesitant in chasing our dreams and goals, and slow to become our best future selves, all because of fear of the criticism we may receive?

When we focus on what "critics" may say about our work, we allow space for that negative, stifling voice inside of our thoughts. The self-doubting one that normally kills our creativity and tells you to keep all that magic waiting inside of you hidden.

Finnish composer Jean Sibelius said it best when discussing critics and their effect on our performances.

"Never pay attention to what critics say. Remember, a statue has never been set up in honour of a critic."

We must also be aware that being too keen to accept or search for praise can also open us up to the pain of receiving criticism.

We can't let praise inflate our egos and allow our pride to bathe in the glory of another's opinion just because they tell us what we want to hear, just as we cannot let the critics tear down all our beliefs in our abilities and possibilities that may await.

It's a double-edged blade.

But criticism can serve a valuable purpose when it is delivered and received correctly. We must be willing and ready to accept it in its greatest form when it is offered.

As philosopher Michel DuMontaigne said, "We need very strong ears to hear ourselves judged frankly, and because there are few who can endure frank criticism without being stung by it, those who venture to criticise us perform a remarkable act of friendship. For to undertake to wound or offend a man for his own good is to have a healthy love for him."

A great friend is someone who cares for us enough that they would risk our opinion of them as they give their criticism to facilitate us to be a better version of ourselves.

As we focus on reframing words and our interpretation of them, how can we, like Du Montaigne says, use this criticism for our own good without taking offence?

Or how can we offer criticism to those we love in a way that will help them improve without causing hurt, pain or conflict?

Let's look at some examples.

If I deliver a public talk, providing content for personal development and mindset shifts, and I receive comments that I perceive as criticism of my content at the end of the course, I will likely struggle to embrace the comments positively.

I would likely find myself on the back foot, acting defensively upon hearing people criticise the content I had worked so diligently on.

How difficult would it be to hear criticism and then act on it, improving my content and using it to improve?

Also, let's look at it from an audience perspective. What would they come up with when asked to offer criticism?

If you were asked to give criticism, what would you come up with?

You would likely be searching for things you didn't like. Something that you found off.

You would likely dig deep to find something, even if there weren't anything you specifically disliked.

If you are a business owner, CEO, Director, Manager, coach or work with a team and you want them to implement your ideas whilst improving how they perform, going all guns blazing, telling them how you have criticisms of how they do things is only going to, at the least, make them instantly defensive, if not offended, and closed off to listening to your ideas, never mind implementing change into their values or work ethic.

But instead, to get the most value, let us change the word and reframe it as: feedback.

It provides us with all the benefits of criticism without it causing us to feel defensive or picked on.

The honesty. The opportunities to listen and see our content from another perspective. It allows us to open doors, create more, serve more and be more.

Feedback is defined as, "Information about reactions to a product, a person's performance of a task, which is used as a basis for improvement."

What a marked difference when we compare the two descriptions of criticism and feedback.

They are so similar in meaning but different in how we understand them.

The big takeaway here is the last eight words.

"Which is used as a basis for improvement."

Whereas criticism is about disapproval, faults, and mistakes, in feedback we see how the outcome of receiving feedback is positive as it provides an opportunity for growth.

Therein lies a significant clue into the power of our perception. Instead of viewing comments as personal attacks, we are able to see the truth in the comments and build from them, utilising them constructively.

When we head into our lesson on growth mindset in chapter thirteen, we will see how much feedback can play a pivotal role in our success.

"Okay, I'll try."

"Do or do not. There is no try."

Yoda

Any Star Wars fans will recognise this quote instantly and be taken back to the scene in the film.

The line is spoken by the tiny, eight-hundred-year-old Jedi master Yoda in response to his student, Luke Skywalker, as he teaches him how to use the force.

The force lesson in the scene is that of telekinesis (moving things with thought) as Luke aims to lift his X-wing starfighter spaceship from the swamp it crash-landed into.

As Luke's ship sinks lower into the swamp, a dejected Luke proclaims, "Oh no, we'll never get it out now."

"So certain are you?' Master Yoda sighs in response. "Always with you. It cannot be done." (A little fixed mindset from a Jedi master, but we'll let it go this time.)

"Hear you nothing that I say?" Yoda continues.

Luke replies with a tone of self-pity in his voice: "Master, moving stones around is one thing. This is totally different."

"No!" Yoda interjects. "No different. Only different in your mind, you must *unlearn* what you have learned."

"Alright, I'll give it a try," Luke pessimistically replies.

"No," the master responds. "Try not. *Do or do not. There is no try*."

Luke then goes on to *try*, lifting the X-wing out of the swamp slightly until he fails and quits, moaning to his master how he asks him of the impossible.

Master Yoda then proceeds to lift the X-wing from the swamp and back onto solid ground.

"I don't believe it!" Luke exclaims.

"And that is why you fail," Yoda replies.

I didn't realise the profound effect that conversation would have on me when I watched it over the years.

How many times have we heard, I'll give it a try?

Anyone with children or who coaches youngsters will have heard it when forcing them to try new things, like eating vegetables or a new activity.

"Ok, I'll try it. See, I don't like it."

Before the food has even touched their lips.

How often have we told it to ourselves? Going somewhere. Meeting someone. Learning something.

"I'll try."

But we know deep down. We know we'll hate it. We know we'll fail.

So we will "try it," but we won't succeed.

When we look at the word's meaning, we can see why it instils this feeling in us. Try: "To make an attempt or effort."

Just reading the description insinuates an outcome of failure or an unsuccessful process.

"I can't believe it," Luke said as he watched his master lift the starfighter from the swamp.

He didn't think it was possible. That is why he "tried." And *that* is why he failed.

We don't try.

We *do*.

BUT I CAN'T

In my experience coaching kids, I often hear this a lot.

"I can't." Yet, one of the magical things about coaching the younger generation is that they're generally quicker to shake off these limiting beliefs than adults are.

Introduce them to a challenging task, and their first reaction is usually, "I can't." But as we'll explore in chapter thirteen on growth mindset, adding just one extra word can make all the difference.

Adults, too, often let negative self-talk dominate when faced with new and daunting tasks. We fret over how we'll look if we try something unfamiliar, afraid of appearing foolish or uninformed. It's an odd paradox, isn't it? We're hesitant to learn new things precisely because we don't already know them.

Epictetus, the Stoic philosopher, hit the nail on the head: "If you wish to improve, be content to appear foolish and stupid."

Embarking on anything new—be it a hobby, a sport, or an instrument—often triggers that internal chorus of, "I can't." In my years of coaching, especially in physical training, this reaction is quite common, strangely enough, with activities like cartwheels. People's instinct is to retreat, claiming, "I can't."

The trick to moving past this mental barrier? Add one simple word: "Yet."

"I can't, yet."

This single word is a game-changer. It grants us permission to progress, to develop a plan tailored to our own pace. It acknowledges our current limitations while highlighting our potential for growth, given the right effort and mindset.

CHAPTER 12
TAKE ACTION

"Action cures fear. Indecision fuels it."

David J Schwarz

We have covered in depth the different states of fight or flight and rest and digest, but there is an often-overlooked state regarding fear—the freeze state.

We've explored the body's physical reactions to threats, but how often do we talk about freezing in place?

Think about a deer caught in headlights— frozen, unable to move. It's an image most of us recognize. This phenomenon isn't just limited to animals; we humans freeze too. Ever given a speech and felt like you were glued to the spot? This isn't uncommon; the best man at a wedding often feels the same way, struggling to articulate thoughts when it's speech time.

This physical freeze usually stems from fear— fear of failure, performance anxiety, or in the case of the deer, not being seen by predators. Yet, what about non-physical threats? Freezing can be mental as well.

Ever felt paralysed when making an important decision? Be it seizing a business opportunity, facing a job interview, or asking someone out, we often freeze in fear. Our mind spins imaginary failure scenarios, deepening our apprehension. We ponder: Should I? Shouldn't I? What if?

The fear of indecision can be suffocating. Yet, when we confront our fear and take steps, even small ones, the paralysis starts to melt away. Facing challenges head-on, we find a way—over, under, or around obstacles.

Avoiding procrastination is crucial, particularly when it masks perfectionism. How many art pieces remain unfinished because they aren't 'perfect'?

That book you have been writing for the last five years, but the perfect paragraph eludes you, so it sits still on the desk, waiting to be finished.

So, when crippled with perfection paralysis, how can we overcome it?

We apply our best.

MY BEST

We can always control our output.

We can be sure that, at that moment, we gave our absolute best.

That we didn't hold anything back and that we went all in each time.

As a coach to some exceptional athletes, I ensure they know they are always in charge of their output.

I have them question themselves: "Is this my best?"

Simple.

Effective.

It carries across everything we do. After all, how you do anything is how you do everything.

If we are training to be healthy, fit, and strong at our local gym, we don't need to train like professional athletes, but we would do well to give our best at every session. To give all we can to best achieve our goals.

Imagine a stressful environment with a bit of pressure; let's imagine we are preparing for a job interview.

We can sit panicked, worrying about imagined outcomes and whether we'll get the job, wasting hours fretting about how we will appear to our potential employers and making a fool of ourselves.

There's a simple plan to eradicate these fears and anxieties: Do your best now in preparation.

Read about the company. Do your research. Ask questions. Find answers. Ready your clothes. Plan your journey. Plan your preparation.

All in advance. If the worrying, anxious thought grabs hold, interrupt it, and stop it in its tracks by asking yourself:

"Have I done my best?"

WHAT IF

As a fighter, those sleepless nights of waking up at two am, with my mind racing about imagined outcomes and possible scenarios seemed unique to me and me alone.

I would lie in bed, fast asleep. As I rolled to turn over and get comfortable, a voice would creep through to my consciousness.

"What if?" It would whisper. "What if you were to lose?'

Then I would be wide awake, my heart racing as I lay in bed.

"Yeah, what if I were to lose?"

If I lose this fight, all my previous victories have been for nothing. All of my hard work and disciplined action wasted because I won't get to the next part of my career, my next big fight.

I wouldn't have my sponsor. I wouldn't have money. I wouldn't be able to compete.

I wouldn't . . .

I can't . . .

Sleeping becomes an issue when these thoughts run around your head, and you don't know how to calm or stop them.

Our overactive thoughts and visualisations put our bodies in to fight or flight mode, not the much-needed rest and digest parasympathetic state, which is imperative at nighttime. This makes it impossible to get the much-needed rest and recovery.

The day after a night like that my training and preparation would take a hit because I was so tired. This would take its toll on my confidence, then, in turn, affect my sleep in this continuing, doubt-filled, fear-based cycle. I was too tired to train at my best without adequate recovery, leaving me feeling more anxious at night, and the cycle would continue.

The issue with the doubting voice was that I allowed it a little control. I allowed it to gain traction. I allowed it to converse with me.

In doing so, its self-doubt ricocheted around my mind and thoughts, infecting all it touched with negativity.

It wasn't only on sleepless nights, either.

Before the big fights or walking out to thousands of people, I could be hitting pads in the warm-up area with my coach, and the voice would pop up.

"How are your lungs feeling, Tom? They seem a little tired and tight."

"Are they?"

They certainly feel a little tighter; I would then think:

"Your legs feeling heavy, Tom?"

Oh man, they are, too!

"Are you sure you're fit enough to fight this guy? Have you done enough?"

And that question, right there, is where all the power lies.

HAVE YOU DONE ENOUGH?

In all my coaching duties, I ensure this concept is wholeheartedly and thoroughly understood. We call it dotting every *I* and crossing every *T*.

Over the course of a fighter's "camp" (where they give absolute focus on training) for a competition or event, they would, on average, plan to peak at the end of around eight weeks, in time for the upcoming event.

There are many variables an athlete or fighter must consider in the active run-up to a competition, contest, or fight: their nutrition, strength work, speed, and agility, rehab, mental conditioning, road work, sparring or skill acquisition.

Sometimes it's easy to skip out on some of these things, especially when you're feeling a little sorry for yourself, or you're tired and a bit low.

But these are the days the "voice" remembers.

Those days you had a bit of self-pity and quit in you.

Some of the Is didn't get dotted, and the Ts didn't have their crosses; deep down, we knew it, but we tried to convince ourselves.

We didn't do what we said we would.

We didn't do what we needed to.

We gave ourselves an excuse.

We didn't give our best.

Come fight day. Event day. Performance day. Interview day. Race day. Meeting day.

We get asked, in preparation, *"Have you done enough?"*

Now we think back to those days we didn't put in those miles on the road. Those days we made incorrect food choices. The days we ignored our coach's advice, those days we didn't prepare.

And we half answer the voice back meekly: "No, maybe I didn't."

And that's all it takes for it to take hold.

Doubt is now in the building and within our thoughts.

We now question ourselves and our abilities, our deservedness, our worthiness.

The outcome may now be different.

"Our doubts are traitors, and make us lose the good we oft might win, by fearing to attempt."

William Shakespeare

When doubt takes hold, it can be debilitating. It will ruin all best-laid plans if we let it.

But how do we stop that voice, or at least dampen it to a controllable level?

We take charge.

I know I can't control the outcome of a competition, test, exam, or business deal.

I don't get to decide if my ideas are a success, but the one thing I can control, that I know will affect my outcome is *giving my best.*

If I gave my best at every turn, every session, every meal, then what more is possible?

If you are to ask yourself, "Have you done enough?"

Be sure you can answer: "I did my best."

"Some things are in our control and others not. Things in our control are opinion, pursuit, desire, aversion, and, in a word whatever are our own actions. Things not in our control are body, property, reputation, command and in one word, whatever are not our actions."

Epictetus, Enchiridion

CHAPTER 13
EMPLOY A GROWTH MINDSET

"I haven't failed. I have just found ten thousand ways that didn't work."

Thomas Edison

Do you believe we are who we are and that is set in stone?

Do you think we cannot change?

Do you feel our lot in life is predetermined?

That we can either inherently do something or we can't?

Or do you think that we are capable of pretty much anything?

That we can learn and continue learning skills throughout our lives as we develop and hone our abilities over the years?

The first opinion is referred to as a fixed mindset. The latter is known as a growth mindset.

Starting in the 1980s, Dr. Carol Dweck began studying how people approach setbacks, challenges, and learning experiences. Through her research, she posited that people's beliefs about their abilities are pivotal in shaping their behaviour and achievements.

Dr. Dweck identified two distinct mindsets—the above-mentioned growth mindset and fixed mindset.

Oftentimes a fixed mindset obstructs people's growth by limiting accountability. Believing that you either can or can't do something prevents you from even trying or exposing yourself to new challenges. A growth mindset, on the other hand, allows precisely was its name suggests: growth.

With a growth mindset, we may admit to not knowing something, but we're also committing to the idea that we can constantly improve if we only allow ourselves the opportunity to be taught.

When we employ a growth mindset, we realise that through each challenge we face, regardless of the outcome, we create an opportunity and environment conducive to growth. Success or failure in relation to any single task is irrelevant because we know that our experience and the lessons therein are the keys to our desires.

One of my many shortcomings as an athlete and entrepreneur years ago, in hindsight, was not consistently applying the growth mindset to all aspects of my career. To give myself some credit, I did use a growth mindset with great success in some areas, but we are capable of having both a fixed and growth mindset on differing situations and I recall a definite point in particular that stands out in my memory when I had a fixed mindset.

Each fight during my competition days felt like the most crucial thing in the world. I understand that for others, it was just a fight, but for me, it was all-consuming. I felt that each fight needed a predetermined outcome, setting the stage for the next fight, the next opportunity, or a bigger show. Unfortunately, this mindset only created unnecessary pressure, negatively impacting my performance.

Had I known how to employ a growth mindset then, I would have focused on continual improvement throughout my 15-year career. Instead, I saw my failures as catastrophic, not realizing they were part of a broader learning process.

A huge aspect of the growth mindset is embracing challenges as opportunities for personal growth. This concept is similar to facing your fears for what they will make of you. Public speaker, motivator, and author Jim Rohn phrased it best: "Do it for what it will make of you to achieve it." Rather than striving to become a millionaire for the things you can buy, consider what the journey to that wealth will build within you. Think about the knowledge and skills you'd acquire along the way.

People with a fixed mindset shy away from challenges. They feel diminished, threatened, and are reluctant to risk appearing foolish or uninformed. The fear of judgment from others causes them to hold back or even pretend to know it all already. How often have you heard people defensively say, "Yeah, I know," even when it's clear they don't? Such pretense hinders growth because these individuals never ask questions, fearful of appearing foolish. As the great Stoic philosopher Epictetus said, "If you wish to improve, be content to be thought foolish and stupid."

People with a growth mindset understand that intelligence and skill are not fixed traits but can be developed through dedication and hard work. They know that failure is neither fatal nor final; instead, it offers lessons and opportunities. They willingly make mistakes because they recognise that's how progress occurs.

Remember being in school when someone would teach you something new, and you'd pretend to know it already? Such pretense to save face prevents you from ever really learning. This same mentality persists in our work lives. People often pretend to know how to perform specific tasks rather than asking for help, and as a result, they perform them incorrectly.

In Brazilian Jiu-Jitsu, the objective is to submit your opponent by placing them in a hold. The act of "tapping out" signifies a submission. This sport serves as an excellent example of how making mistakes is integral to growth. Each submission you experience teaches you how to avoid it in the future. But for that, you must be willing to make mistakes.

Years ago, during my professional career, the man who later became my teacher arrived at our gym in the UK. While training together, he caught me in a head-and-arm choke. Eager to learn, I asked him to repeat the move. My Brazilian teammates found it odd, but I was willing to make that mistake repeatedly to learn how to avoid it.

Many of the lessons learned from years of combat sports translate to day-to-day life. The adversity faced today helps build resilience for tomorrow. This is why it's essential to embrace challenges and ask questions, no matter how "stupid" they may seem. Remember, "There are no stupid questions, only stupid answers."

Feeling okay with not knowing something is crucial for skill development and achieving growth. With a fixed mindset, talent is perceived as innate. However, a growth mindset shows us that we can learn anything through dedication and practice.

INSPIRED OR ENVIOUS

How many people do you find inspiring?

Do you look at successful people and think, *I can do that with the correct planning and work*, or do you think, *there's no way I ever could*?

Being honest, do you sometimes feel envious of others' successes? Maybe people you know.

A family member.

A colleague.

A friend.

Do they create feelings of inadequacy or jealousy deep inside you?

When others speak of their achievements, do you try to belittle their successes?

This is a fixed mindset.

If this is you (a round of applause for being honest as there are more of us than we would like to admit feel this way) then try to realise that you, too, are capable of achieving just the same and more and that those around you aren't showing off but showing you what is possible.

Understand that all these people who succeed, who achieve what they set out to, are no different from you.

They have days of self-doubt.

The nights of fearful thoughts.

But *they* push forward toward their North Star, toward their goal, because they have faith and know it is possible. They know that if others can do it, so can they.

If you're unsure how they attained success, ask them what they did.

Allow them to inspire you to see precisely what is possible when the correct mindset is adopted, plans are implemented, and the right action is taken.

OPEN UP TO NEW EXPERIENCES

Employing a growth mindset can sometimes leave us feeling vulnerable.

We close ourselves off from new experiences and keep ourselves hidden away from a fear of looking foolish to others.

It can be the same when falling in love.

When you meet someone, it's easy not to give your all to a blossoming relationship for fear of a broken heart. It's easy not to allow someone to love you fully because you're afraid of being so vulnerable. But in the long run, it's much harder to have never felt that love at all. To have never trusted enough. To have never connected deeply.

Think about all the things a fixed mindset might take away from us in life.

Job interviews never attempted.

A boy never asked out for coffee.

A business never built.

A life never altered.

If this is resonating with you right now, make a plan to go try something different, something new. This idea that you're keeping yourself "safe" is only holding you back.

FAILURE IS THE FERTILISER TO MY SUCCESS

"Failure is simply the opportunity to begin again, this time, more intelligently."

Henry Ford

With a fixed mindset, once we fail, that is it. We're done. We tell our selves stories that sound like this:

"I'm stupid."

"I'm a failure."

"I'm not doing that again."

"I'm embarrassed."

We take the verb *I failed* and then create our identity with it and make it a noun.

I am a failure.

But this statement couldn't be further from the truth.

Failures are precisely what we need to be able to learn the correct ways of doing things. Like Benjamin Franklin once said, "The things that hurt, instruct." All of the greats fail. All the successful people learn from their failures.

If I were to ask most people to name the greatest basketball player of all time, they would likely say Michael Jordan.

Now, I am sure that no one would label him a failure, and yet he talks of failing multiple times, knowing that failure is part of the path towards success:

"I've missed more than nine thousand shots in my career. I've lost almost 300 games. Twenty-six times, I have been trusted to take the game winning shot and missed. I've failed over and over and over again in my life. And that is why I *succeed.*"

With the use of a growth mindset, we can continue towards our goals and accept failure and making mistakes as part of the process of getting there.

"Success is the ability to go from failure to failure without losing your enthusiasm."

Winston Churchill

Churchill said the above during World War II when he was battling Nazi Germany. At the peak of the highest risk of everything: war.

It's the same in business, sports, life.

Learn from the lessons and keep pushing forward.

Each mistake, each failure, every time we think we have fallen all provide us with the opportunity to grow and learn and become better than ever.

All of my mistakes fuelled me to be better. Failing is in every success story. At the time, during my MMA career, I didn't realise it. I was too closed off. But every loss led to lessons I would never have been exposed to and opportunities that offered me little choice other than growth. It wasn't even that the lessons were instant, many times they weren't, but they provided me with knowledge that helped me not only in my fighting career, most notably, within my coaching role.

That is why I embrace my mistakes. That is how I know that failure is the fertiliser to my success.

It not only provides us with new lessons, methods, and ways, but renewed desires that reinvigorate us to go again.

Have you been able to utilise your past failures as lessons and ways to assist you in achieving all that you desire? If not, it's time to start now.

FOCUS ON THE PROCESS

Goal setting is an extremely important aspect of achieving success.

When we go grocery shopping, a list is important, especially when we have specifics in mind. Otherwise, it can be easy to overspend, buying things we didn't even want or need, and often (always for me) forgetting the main thing we went for.

Starting with the end in mind is possibly one of the most significant habits, taken from coveys the seven habits of highly effective people, you can adopt in putting a growth mindset to work around goal setting. Simply put, work out what you *want*, then work backwards from there until you reach where you're currently at. Then build a plan to bridge the gap from where you're at to the focused outcome, moving through each point until you reach your goal. Amazing stuff.

I mention this now about goals and starting with the end in mind so as not to cause any confusion whilst discussing the growth mindset lesson of focusing on the process.

Focusing on the process allows us to be on the journey, learn, and adapt as we go. Focusing solely on outcomes relies on too many variables to create happiness or success.

The sport of MMA, like many sports and endeavours, has you start at the bottom and work your way upwards.

You begin competing on small stages, in gyms mainly, then you progress to a local hall, then bigger sports halls, then more prominent venues, then venues around the world, until ultimately you fight in an arena or stadium live around the world in front of thousands of fans and even more watching at home.

It's the standard procedure that roughly eighty per cent of combat sports athletes would have followed in the past and still do follow today.

It can work exceptionally well. It helps to develop a career as the athlete becomes accustomed to not only a step up in competition but also the rise in production and fan interaction.

Understanding it as a process to allow yourself to develop is the key.

The issue is, as athletes, the majority of us think about the end goal and getting to it as soon as possible. We rarely enjoy the present moment of building ourselves on the journey.

When I fought, I never allowed myself to enjoy the process.

I knew I would end up at the UFC.

I thought I would be champion.

Now I coach to help others realise the mistakes I made in ignoring the process. I focused too much on reaching the UFC. At the time, I needed it, as my process of getting to the UFC was a long one that was short-lived.

Instead of always looking at the outcome of reaching the UFC, I should have been enjoying every minute of the process. Taking it all in and understanding that each day was a day to improve myself. I created undue pressure on myself to meet this fantastic goal of competing in the premier fighting organisation, which led me to become damaged, hurt, and fall out of love with the sport.

I would fight and compete on the local and global martial arts scene, always believing that I *must* perform and win. Like an old treasure map, I would lay out the path to gold in my head, inadvertently creating pressure on myself that would only lead to disappointment and hurt. I would mark off in my mind each step, when I win here, that will then get me to there, where I will win here, and then I will get the call to that spot there.

Now I know that the process is where the magic happens. The process is where life happens.

The process of learning.

The process of struggling and of hardships.

The process of growth

Each part of our lives and careers are all part of a journey leading to a destination. When we reach the destination, we feel we *need* to reach, we make a plan to head to a new one. But it's important to understand that the man who loves the journey will always walk farther than the man who needs the destination.

Enjoy your process.

That is all there ever truly is.

CHAPTER 14
CHANGING STATES

"Everyone thinks of changing the world, but no one thinks of changing himself."

Leo Tolstoy

To keep it simple, a state refers to your mood.

Feeling low and depressed is a state, and more than likely, it's one we would wish to avoid when we are in it. But when we are in this low state, it can be really difficult to pull ourselves out of it.

That fearful state can be even harder to escape when we create scary thoughts and worrisome outcomes with our creative imaginations. We willingly sit feeling anxious or depressed, feeling sorry for ourselves and staying in a state that produces nothing positive or productive for us.

But we can actively decide to change that state when we feel overwhelmed, anxious, or low by performing certain state-altering activities.

The following are my favorite practices for resetting our mind-body connection and moving from the state we're in, to the sate we want to be in.

POSTURE

When we think of someone as fearful, we can visualise them lacking confidence through their posture—the way they stand and carry themselves. Shoulders rolled and hunched forward, their heads looking down to the floor. Their arms hang heavy by their sides, dragging their feet along the floor as they walk. We can even make ourselves feel disempowered by standing or sitting in this way, letting it adversely affect our mood.

Whenever I get the opportunity to coach children in class, my first action is to have them all stand in the correct posture. They all line up, standing differently depending on their day. Some have hands in pockets; some have arms folded. Shoulders slumped, looking down, depending on their dominant thoughts that day.

They all get told to stand straight; they already feel a little bigger. Chin up, stand proud and let people see you. Shoulders back, feel strong and confident. Arms by your side and take your hands out of your pockets.

Now they feel ready to perform. Ready to listen. Ready to be coached and prepared to feel strong.

It's precisely the same for us. Sat at our desk feeling a little miserable or low, hunching over into a depressive state, yet all it takes is a little straightening of the back, standing up, and moving to invigorate us again.

MOVE

As we alter our posture, we can also begin to move with purpose. Lift ourselves from sitting, chin up, chest out, and move. Take a walk, get some fresh air, and feel the blood flow improve your state.

Walking can even be utilised in meditation. As we walk, we can learn to enter a meditative state. Physical exercise cannot be understated for not only its beneficial effects on our bodies but also its massive positive effect on our state.

Running, lifting weights, and enjoying a sport or martial art like jiu-jitsu or boxing can massively help to change a state. If you're unable to be as active as you would like due to injury or ailment, aim to try for a little walk outdoors if possible and see what a difference it can make.

During one of the lowest points in my life, I had been badly hurt with a spinal injury that had also prevented me from using my arm for a long time. Even doing my coaching job was extremely difficult, and to top it off, I received a terrible knee injury that forced me to be bed-bound.

The collection of injuries, surgeries, and other stressful factors caused me to be in a constant, fearful, depressed state. Uncertainty was running riot in my thoughts, and I was in constant, unending pain, which led me to develop an addiction to nerve-suppressing drugs and prescription opioids just to try to mask a small part of the agony I faced daily.

I had to take my pain medication everywhere I went in case I needed it. I was terrified to be without it at my side in case of an emergency flare-up, but I knew things had to change.

As soon as I could return to walking, I started my rehab intensely. I made sure I didn't go too hard too soon but started with a mobility program focused solely on rehab and recovery, emphasizing the smaller muscles first, which can stabilise and support. Then, as my confidence grew, so did my training and eventually my muscles again.

SMILE

"A smile is a curve that sets everything straight."

Phyllis Diller

What came first, the chicken or the egg?

It's a question that likely has no answer and is irrelevant, but I ask because a state change or a smile is very similar. Many people assume we smile in response to something happening that we like, and then we feel good in response to that event.

But what if actually smiling made the difference? Putting the smile on first, irrespective of mood, can really help make a difference in how you feel. Even if you haven't yet received great news or seen something to make you smile, put that smile on your face anyway and see how it alters your feeling.

It is thought that Darwin initially introduced this idea in his book *The Expressions of Emotions in Man and Animals*, and it has continued to be studied and theorized by many over the years, up until as recently as 2008.

"The facial feedback hypothesis" involved researchers intending to test the theory that our face can dictate our mood: i.e., if we frown, we feel more anger or upset, or if we smile, we feel happier.

The study conducted at the Max Planck Institute compared women's emotional responses through the use of a brain scanner to see the effect frowning had on the brain.

The women were asked to imitate a photograph of an angry face as their brains were scanned. During the scan, their brains showed activity in both sides of the amygdala, the part of the brain that helps regulate emotion and encode memories. Then they injected the women's faces with Botox, immobilising their muscles and preventing them from frowning. When they redid the study, placing the women in the brain scanner and asking them to imitate an angry face after the Botox treatment, the scans showed significantly less activity in the left side of the amygdala.

Maybe our parents were right when they would ask, "Are you happy?"

And you'd reply, "Yeah."

"Well, tell your face that then."

Hilarious, I know.

But these studies show how imperative the emotions we display on our faces are in affecting the emotions we feel inside our brains. I'm not saying that smiling will make everything okay, but reminding ourselves to sit with a smile certainly can't do us harm and may, as the studies suggest, help us feel actively happier.

Many of us seem to have this strange misconception that negative thinking is realistic, whereas positive thinking is wishy-washy and pretend. It's as if we think frowning and being miserable is the way we are meant to be.

Allow yourself a few minutes of smiling and see how it affects your mood. Just sit there for two minutes and put a smile on that face; see how it makes you feel.

Not only will a nice smile make you feel better, but you will look better, too.

Smiles are contagious. If you see someone without a smile, give them yours.

"Sometimes, your joy is the source of your smile, but sometimes, your smile can be the source of your joy."

Thich Nhat Hanh

SELF-TALK AND THOUGHTS

How often do you keep track of the thoughts and messages that pop up in your head? Do you feel that you are in charge of these thoughts, or do they edge their way in and alter your mood on their own? What does your internal dialogue say to you? Is it empowering or disempowering?

As we touched upon in the chapter on growth mindset, do you see yourself as defined by the failures you make? Does your internal voice belittle your self-esteem? Ensuring that our thoughts and beliefs are happy and productive is essential for living confidently, without fear and anxiety. Our subconscious thoughts have been proven to be instrumental in shaping our belief systems.

If we constantly deride ourselves, calling ourselves names for acting incorrectly sometimes, making mistakes, or failing tasks, then all we are doing is forcing ourselves to operate at a much lower level of competency than we are able and capable of achieving.

"The happiness in your life depends upon the quality of your thoughts."

Marcus Aurelius

How can we alter our thoughts to make them kinder and, in turn, more conducive to success? Firstly, when a negative thought arises, it's not the end of the world. It happens to everyone. Don't sit there getting upset, annoyed, or frustrated with yourself; instead, use it and embrace it as a reminder—as a trigger.

In meditation, the goal isn't to have no thoughts at all but to recognize them when they appear. A common misconception about starting a meditation practice is that you're supposed to sit and think of nothing. This is incredibly difficult; the more you try, the more elusive it becomes.

Naturally, thoughts and images will pop up as we sit quietly in meditation. Those who believe that we shouldn't have any thoughts during meditation often get frustrated and abandon the practice. Meditation is a skill like any other: you learn it, and then you practice it with discipline as often as possible. You don't compete with anyone; you aim to enjoy your practice and maintain discipline in your study.

The key to excellent meditative practice is acknowledging that thoughts will arise. Allow the thought to pass by, acknowledge its appearance, but understand that it isn't important at this moment. Then, shift your focus back to your anchor, which could be your breath, a count, or a mantra.

With practice, you can use these thoughts as triggers to return to your meditative state. You don't chide or judge yourself; you're grateful for the reminder and tell yourself, "I'm not thinking about that right now; I will release that thought and return to my breath count."

During everyday life, our thoughts operate in much the same way. Instead of succumbing to negative or defeatist self-talk, use it as a reminder to engage in positive self-talk or even self-praise. For instance, when you think, "You're not smart enough for that job," don't accept it. Use this moment as a catalyst for change. Re-record your self-talk with empowering words that make you feel powerful and conjure images of strength.

By altering the narrative, you strengthen the habit of thinking empowering thoughts. You turn your negative self-talk into positive reinforcement, allowing it to trigger upbeat thoughts and empowering emotions every time they appear.

Self-pity and victimization serve no one, especially when you know you're capable of more. It takes courage and discipline to transform negatives into positives, to change "I can't" to "I will."

Remember to own your victories, not as flukes or lucky moments, but as evidence of your limitless potential. Many of us allow our failures to define us while downplaying our successes. Instead, let every win be a reminder of your ability to succeed, proof that you are infinitely capable.

GRATITUDE

"I cried because I had no shoes until I met a man who had no feet."

Helen Keller

We have already covered gratitude extensively in the previous chapters, but I know it is such a vital feeling that it deserves another quick mention in this chapter on altering states.

It's extremely difficult, if not impossible, to be fearful, afraid, sad ,or depressed when we allow gratitude a space in our hearts. To feel both emotions simultaneously, negative and positive, is a skill very few could muster. But sometimes, it can be challenging to find gratitude and show it.

That negative victim voice can try to keep us upset or afraid with the things it says, like:

"What have I got to be grateful for?"

"It's easy for others to say to be happy/positive/grateful."

It's easier not to find something to be grateful for and to remain bitter. It's easier to remain in self-pity and act like only you have faced hardship.

The truth is we all have problems and have, at some point in our lives, played the victim role, but there are always things to be grateful for. When you find them and truly feel them, your state will change.

GIVING AND SERVITUDE

Whenever you delve into the financial habits of those deemed successful, you observe similar traits and patterns many seem to follow.

One is their charitable and philanthropic work, their propensity for giving. Whether this is financial, charitable donations, or gifts of time in helping toward a goal or achievement or mentoring a youngster—the gift of giving is a fantastic tool to help shift states.

Avoiding the discussions and opinions on whether it is a selfless act or not, giving feels good; there's no denying it.

It's a win-win situation.

Helping those in need feels good. Being there for those in a time of need feels great.

It helps others and makes you feel good, too.

When feeling low, make a plan to help someone who needs you. See how you can live in servitude of others. See how that helps you to feel about yourself.

The fantastic motivational speaker and author Zig Ziglar used to say, "You can have everything in life you want if you will just help other people get what they want."

GOALS

Whenever we have something we want to achieve in our lives, setting specific goals and targets is crucial. Whether in our careers or personal lives, having clear aims is imperative for living our best lives. As Seneca wisely said, "Without a ruler, you can't make the crooked straight."

When we feel upbeat and positive, setting goals becomes easier. We can then create a plan to achieve them over a predetermined timeline.

For example, if your goal is to play the piano, simply stating it is too vague. Questions arise: How proficiently do you want to play? Do you wish to play a few songs from memory for entertainment, or do you aspire to read music and play a wide repertoire?

Achieving proficiency in any domain—especially something as complex as music—requires time, patience, discipline, and consistency. Goals need to be broken down into smaller, manageable objectives. Learning to master an instrument might take a lifetime and learning to read music could take years but taking it one step at a time makes the process enjoyable and the goal attainable.

Another example I often encounter is the desire to read more books. Reading is a powerful tool for self-improvement, yet many people rarely open a book. The goal of reading more is commendable but too vague to establish a sustainable habit. This lack of specificity can lead to feelings of inadequacy and frustration.

However, setting a tangible target, such as reading ten pages a day, allows you to see real progress. If ten pages are too ambitious, scale it down. Choose a daily thought-provoking book or adjust the number of pages to your comfort level. Stick to a set time each day, and watch the habit form. Reading ten pages a day means finishing most average-length books in two to three weeks—adding potentially ten to twelve books a year to your reading list.

Consistent work towards our goals not only brings us closer to achieving them but also improves our overall well-being. Although it's easy to get distracted by our mobile devices, which can exacerbate feelings of inadequacy, a little discipline can go a long way.

Completing even one task on our daily list brings us one step closer to our goal, positively impacting our mood and self-worth.

IF MUSIC BE THE FOOD OF LOVE

I love listening to music. All kinds. Except maybe the hardcore dance type music with an M.C shouting all throughout it, which I'm not so keen on. But I would say my music style is very widespread, and I enjoy lots.

I am, however, cautious of what I listen to often.

Here's why.

I speak to many people about changing states and altering how we feel, but not many mention the effects of music.

There are multiple ways in which music can make us feel. We can listen to a piece of music, take in and absorb the lyrics, or feel the tone, chords, and intended mood of the music and the emotional intent behind the song.

As well as the music creating an emotional state and feeling within us, we can also link the music to a particular time or place, which triggers those feelings we had then at that remembered moment.

An easy example to prove my point would be a wedding song. Usually, when people get married, they have chosen a song they link to that momentous special day—a song they love that may have prior meaning that will mark the momentous occasion of the couple sharing this special day forever.

Their first dance to a track that they have decided is "their" song.

Now, each time they hear that song, it will always transport them back to that special day when they were in love and marrying the love of their life.

Not only can hearing the song take them back in their mind to that day, but it can also take them back to the same feelings they had on that day, back to their emotional state. With hope, it is a powerful memory that reminds you of a wonderful, loving day, and the song creates a state of joy and happiness within you.

The same is true for feelings of excitement with a song that fires you up and gets you switched on and motivated to move.

A fighter is selective about his walkout track on purpose. They can't just walk out to any music. They need to get the right track that gets them going.

But it can become difficult to listen to that track and not either: A: Feel the need/desire to compete, be physical, be hyped up, or B: Turn it off as quickly as possible as its links to the fight remind you of a horrible performance or the adrenaline has started, placing you in a fight or flight state, and it feels a little overwhelming and strange when you don't know why it's happening.

For fighters/competitors, embracing this reaction can be highly beneficial in utilising the state changes for performance.

Randomly listening to a track like this can also cause what we know as an adrenaline dump, when a shot of adrenaline comes out of the blue from a random stimulus (say a loud noise or somebody's reaction to something). In competition terms, it can be debilitating if you aren't used to feeling this way, so embracing this and exposing ourselves as often as possible can be highly beneficial to our progress in coping with nerves.

Not all music has an associated emotional memory, but all music does have the capacity and ability to alter our state for better or worse.

How often have you felt sad or too emotional after listening to certain songs or artists?

There are particular songs I think are amazing and beautiful works of art, but I choose not to listen to them due to my emotional state after hearing them.

Songs with whiney lyrics, complaining, suffering and how hard life is get turned off most of the time—I don't allow them space in my mind as they embody a victimhood mentality, seemingly seeping into my state if I let it.

How often do we see teenagers upset at the world, filled with angst, listening to music with the same message?

Is it the chicken and the egg again?

Maybe they listen to it because they feel that way, or perhaps they feel that way because they hear it.

I make sure to listen only to songs with empowering lyrics that always put me in a good state, one that makes me feel like I can take on all challenges.

It's easy to feel low, and then it seems inviting to pull ourselves deeper into that sad state by listening to sad music.

I'm sure everyone with a bad break-up likes to put Adele on their headphones and cry in sadness alongside her about losing love. I understand the need sometimes, but when we know we are wallowing in a little self-pity, we can at least decide we don't want to do it anymore and eventually make the active choice to listen to upbeat, positive music.

BREATHWORK

In recent years, breathing has become a hot topic in wellness circles everywhere.

Lots of people take a defensive attitude and say, "I think I know how to breathe. I've been doing it all my life."

But the problem is we can all do it, but lots of us have been doing it incorrectly for a long time.

Let's us begin by asking ourselves how we usually breathe. Do we do it through our mouths or nose?

Breathing shallowly through our mouths, only filling our chests, is not the natural way our bodies were designed to breathe. This way of breathing contributes to various modern health issues, including upper respiratory tract infections and teeth misalignment. Instead, we should strive for nasal breathing—inhaling and exhaling slowly and steadily, filling our bellies with each breath.

When you breathe, let your stomach expand on the inhale and contract slowly on the exhale. Keep your lips sealed and allow your tongue to rest on the roof of your mouth. For a comprehensive tutorial on this essential breathing technique, visit www.TomBlackledge.com.

Nasal breathing is not just a useful practice during focused breathing or meditation; it should be the norm in our day-to-day lives. It serves as a powerful tool for calming the mind, shifting focus, and optimizing health when done correctly.

The medical community has extensively documented the detrimental effects of mouth breathing on our well-being. These include higher dental arches, smaller mouths, crooked or overlapping teeth, dental decay, and increased susceptibility to respiratory illness. Other negative outcomes such as an elevated resting heart rate and reduced oxygen levels are also associated with mouth breathing. Furthermore, sleep apnea—a condition where your breathing sporadically stops and starts during sleep—is linked to mouth breathing, among other factors.

Utilising our nasal cavity for its intended purpose strengthens the muscles involved in our respiratory system. To promote nasal breathing during sleep, experts recommend placing a small piece of medical tape over the lips, helping to keep them sealed throughout the night.

CALMING BREATH TECHNIQUE

When feeling anxious or under pressure, you can use controlled breathing techniques to shift your body into a state of rest and relaxation, activating the parasympathetic nervous system. Before I offer you a couple of routines, remember this golden rule for calming breaths: exhale longer than you inhale. This technique helps lower your heart rate and calms your nervous system.

For instance, you can inhale for four seconds and then exhale for eight seconds—a simple yet effective 4:8 breathing ratio.

To try this, you can either go to www.tomblackledge.com for a guided session or follow these steps. Firstly, lie on your back or sit comfortably and place your right hand on your stomach and your left hand on your chest. Be mindful as you breathe that your left-hand doesn't move much, whereas your right hand, the hand on the stomach, lifts with each inhale and falls with each exhale.

Begin by breathing all your air out and away. Expel the air from your lungs.

Close your mouth, place your tongue on the roof of your mouth, and slowly begin breathing into your belly through your nose.

As you breathe in, count slowly upwards.

1 . . . 2 . . . 3 . . . 4 . . .

Pause

Exhale, now count downwards.

8 . . . 7 . . . 6 . . . 5 . . . 4 . . . 3 . . . 2 . . . 1 . . .

Pause

Inhale

1 . . . 2 . . . 3 . . . 4 . . .

Pause

Exhale slowly

8 . . . 7 . . . 6 . . . 5 . . . 4 . . . 3 . . . 2 . . . 1 . . .

Keep this going until your alarm alerts you that you're finished as you keep your attention on your breath.

BOX BREATHING TECHNIQUE

A slightly more advanced technique but one that is very beneficial to developing focus is referred to as box breathing.

When we do box breathing, we still want to count our inhales and exhales as before, but it also involves holding our breath after both exhalation and inhalation.

As you close your eyes, you want to picture a box in front of you. On each line of this square box, assign an equal amount of time, like the image below.

To keep your first practice simple, we will keep it to a basic four seconds for each line to begin.

4 SECOND INHALE

4 SECOND HOLD

4 SECOND HOLD

4 SECOND EXHALE

The first line of the imaginary square is our breath being in—our inhale—and we do this for four seconds.

The next line is the line down, on our right, and as we travel down this line, we hold on to our inhale with air-filled lungs for the count of four.

As we reach the bottom of this line, we come to our four-second exhale.

We now want to control our breath and make it last four seconds as we travel across this imaginary square line towards our left. Slowly letting our bellies deflate as the air leaves our lungs until we reach the last line.

Then, as we reach our last line, the ascent upwards back to the beginning, we hold our lungs empty.

After our exhale, we sit still with no air in our lungs as we count down from four to one. Then we find ourselves back at the start and start our count from one to four again as we inhale and continue the process.

The holds are simple. They just involve sitting there with or without breath in the lungs.

On your first few goes at this practice, aim for just three minutes total or so to become accustomed to the techniques and timings. It's a simple enough process that, once utilised a few times, it can become highly beneficial to altering states and assisting with better physical health and mental health.

Gradually, over time of developing these simple breath work techniques, you can begin to add in more advanced techniques that are available in various places as well as on my site at www.TomBlackledge.com.

MEDITATION

Oftentimes, meditation and breathwork seemingly get confused as the same practice. While there are many similarities, they are not one and the same.

In this book, I chose to place breathwork first, before meditation, as breathing in the ways described above can really assist with your meditation practice.

Breathwork and the various breathing exercises can and should be used and embraced in times of stress as an instant and demonstrative way to alter your state whenever you feel the onset of anxiety or fearful emotions creeping in during times of stress.

Meditation, however, is done more so as a preventative measure. It is a practice we do daily with discipline whose benefits arise in a myriad of ways, oftentimes subtle and hidden from plain sight. It is embraced as much for its preventative qualities as anything else.

The word meditation practice to the uninitiated can conjure up images of religion and monks chanting, thinking it to be some useless spiritual mumbo jumbo.

However, this couldn't be further from the truth. Regular meditation practice is excellent for providing us with the ability to maintain a calm state while under stressful situations. And it can really benefit us in providing us with the ability to bring our regular state to one of calmness while also remaining alert.

When people think about meditation, many think it is about sitting and having no thoughts, the ability to sit with an empty mind devoid of images, words, or events.

But this is not an accurate representation of what meditation is for most, and it likely adds to most people feeling unable to begin to practice meditation.

It's challenging to sit and have no thoughts. Then, if you try, the more frustrated you seem to get as more thoughts pop up in your mind.

Suddenly thinking you should have a clear mind as you practice meditation brings more frustration as you realise you can't reach some inner Zen.

When you get frustrated at a seemingly impossible task, you decide to abandon it as it feels like too much and appears too difficult.

Like setting goals, we need to be mindful of being able to attain them in bite-sized chunks. Sitting in meditation with no distractions is the long game. So we want to whittle it down to smaller attainable goals.

So, to begin our practice, we sit calmly and comfortably with our eyes closed and focus our attention on our breath.

In for a count and out for a count. Similar in theory to the box breathing we practised earlier.

We use our noses to breathe both in and out, breathing into our bellies in a calm and controlled manner.

We focus all our attention on to our breath, and we will make this our "anchor," a focal point used to minimise the entrance of distraction. Note that I said minimise, not eliminate.

To keep it simple, we think about the breath, the repetition of the inhale and the exhale. This is all we repeat internally to ourselves.

Inevitably though, thoughts will arise as you sit quietly, meditating. The most random things, images, and thoughts will pop up. Past experiences, visions of future events, imagined conversations, and other strange, unrelated thoughts.

What we resist will persist.

When we face these thoughts popping up in our mind, it's imperative we don't allow ourselves to become frustrated and allow negative, defeatist self-talk to arise. Instead, we will use the random thoughts that interrupt as a gift to remind us to go back to our focused practice.

Note the thought. Note you had the thought. We offer gratitude to the thought and then let it go, telling ourselves we will return to that concern after our practice is completed. Then return your thoughts to your breath.

Back to the count.

Back to our meditation.

If a thought interrupts your meditation practice, which it inevitably will, just use this script in a calm, controlling manner.

"Thank you for reminding me about this. I can't currently stay and think about this thing (whatever the thought is) for the current moment in time, but thank you for releasing me and reminding me about my anchor, breath, count, 1 . . . 2 . . . 3 . . . 4 . . ."

This conversation will happen a lot. But every time you return your thought to your breath, you will find it easier to return. Every time you don't judge yourself negatively for the interruption and offer gratitude for the reminder, you will notice your practice continually improves.

There is no set time to practice meditation. Whenever suits you best is fine. Morning, afternoon, or evening—it doesn't matter as long as you can get it to fit into your schedule.

However, as you start your practice, I recommend that you make it a habit for the same time every day. That way, it will slot into your lifestyle, and you will consistently see the improvements not only in your meditation technique but also in the benefits it offers in your day-to-day life.

I get the most benefit from my practice at the same time every night before I go to bed.

The accumulative effects not only help me in my daily life of serenity and calmness but also helps me fall straight to sleep when I get to bed in such a calm and relaxed state.

I also perform a shorter morning routine, which allows me to collect my thoughts before the day, but my evening routine is the most consistent and seemingly most rewarding.

So set a time, develop the routine, and plan to start for just five minutes a day to begin with, as you become accustomed to the practice. Then, over time, you can gradually increase the time spent meditating up to thirty minutes.

CHAPTER 15
CONCLUSION

"An apple a day keeps the doctor away."

There's a saying from a long time ago that eating an apple a day will help keep you healthy and keep you from needing to visit your family doctor frequently.

Throughout this book, I have collected and shown you many ways to push through fear, anxiety and other stumbling blocks that can get in our way.

After spending your valuable time reading this book, the knowledge is now, at a surface level, yours.

But there's a catch.

Just reading the book isn't enough to make those massive changes we require to live the life we are capable of.

You must put the chosen coping mechanisms into practice.

Take action.

Consistently.

The saying isn't seven apples on a Sunday or a few apples here and there when we can be bothered keeps the doctor away.

No, it is an apple a day.

Consistency.

As with most things we want to develop, we need to be consistent.

We don't go to the gym, lift weights one time, expect our physiques to change shape miraculously, and suddenly gain twenty pounds of muscle and lose all of our unwanted fat.

We must develop a consistent routine that will provide us with the greatest opportunity to grow and expand.

The things you have learned in this book are no different. Be disciplined with your actions and purposeful with your practice.

If you are to employ the daily gratitude ritual as your own, be sure to employ it to its full benefit and with full intention daily.

If you want to be able to calm yourself at a moment's notice during times of stress, then be sure to practice your breathwork during times of calm so you have the technique perfected.

If you want to feel calmer throughout the day and sleep better, be sure to diligently practice your meditation every day at the same time.

I hope that you can utilise the mechanisms I have taught you and that they will provide you with the exact help they afforded me and still do provide me and my athletes in our day-to-day lives.

Introduce each method slowly and take your time. You don't need to instantly introduce all the habits to your lifestyle in one go.

If it suits you, choose the methods you feel will benefit you most.

Please keep pushing on through your fears. The dreams you want to achieve, whatever they may be, are possible if you only have a little belief and head in the right direction.

Have faith in yourself and those who want to help you, and you may just surprise yourself when you look back at exactly how far you have come.

There's a lot that can be said about pure determination and a little belief—like the water drop that creates the hole in stone, continued effort and unwavering faith can also penetrate all obstacles.

There is a wonderful poem from a young poet, Erin Hanson, that perfectly encapsulates the theme of this book.

Its message is such a positive and uplifting one and an embodiment of many things I coach that I thought it pertinent and important that as many people as possible should take it in.

"There is freedom waiting for you, on the breezes of the sky, and you ask 'what if I fall?'

Oh but my darling what if you fly?"

Erin Hanson

If you can pass this information on to others to help them, please do, and if I helped you maybe I can help them too, so please send them a link to this book or to my coaching and development website: www.TomBlackledge.com.

Take care.

Printed in Great Britain
by Amazon

41224065R00121